DIANE KEATON
The Story of the Real Annie Hall

12

21 Oct 99

DIANE KEATON
The Story of the Real Annie Hall

JONATHAN MOOR

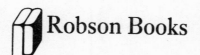 Robson Books

Grateful acknowledgement is made for permission to use: excerpts from articles and reviews that originally appeared in *The New York Times*, permission granted by *The New York Times*; excerpt from an interview with Richard Brooks that appeared in *The Boston Phoenix*, permission granted by *The Boston Phoenix*; excerpt from an interview with Diane Keaton by Gerald L'Ecuyer that appeared in *Interview*, permission granted by *Interview* magazine; excerpt from 'Retribution' by Woody Allen which appeared in *Side Effects*, permission granted by Random House, Inc. New York, copyright © 1975, 1976, 1977, 1979, 1980 by Woody Allen; excerpt from *Still Life* by Diane Keaton, permission granted by Simon & Schuster, copyright © 1983 by Diane Keaton and Marvin Heiferman.

First published in Great Britain in 1990 by Robson Books Ltd, Bolsover House, 5-6 Clipstone Street, London W1P 7EB

Copyright © 1989 Jonathan Moor

British Library Cataloguing in Publication Data
Moor, Jonathan
    Diane Keaton: the story of the real Annie Hall
    1. Cinema films. Acting. Biographies
    I. Title
    791.43′028′0924

ISBN 0 86051 640 7

Printed in Great Britain by Billing & Sons Ltd, Worcester

Contents

*To someone else who always feels the cold, and
who has so much talent.*

With all my love, Jonathan

Acknowledgments

First of all, I have to thank Diane Keaton for not standing in my way when I told her I wanted to write her life story, even though she characteristically didn't understand why I wanted to do it! I hope my reasons will become apparent to her.

Many thanks to my editor Toni Lopopolo, whose continued support and interest made this book such a joy to write. Her encyclopedic knowledge of film helped me put much into perspective and saved me from making a few blunders. I also can't forget her assistant Stacia Friedman for all the help she gave me.

Most of the research could not have been done without the consummate help from the staff of the General Library and Museum of the Performing Arts New York Public Library at Lincoln Center. A special thank you to all of you for your patience with my requests.

Many of my friends in the Hollywood community gave me insight into the making of films and some of them, specifically, into the films Ms. Keaton has made, as they were part of the creative process of making those films.

There are also many people in the New York offices of the major film companies who lent their assistance in my research. I would especially like to thank Bill Kenly and Peter de Rome at Paramount Pictures.

Many people assisted me in digging up photographs to illustrate this portrait of Diane Keaton, and no one was more diligent than Ron Mandlebaum at Photofest who managed to find everything I was searching for, however obtuse, from Keaton's performances over twenty-one years. Thank you.

I am most appreciative of the time and help given to me by staffs of the libraries of Santa Ana High School and Santa Ana College, and especially Bob Blaustone of the theater department of Orange Coast College.

Lastly, I would like to thank my agent Madeleine Morel for everything she has done for me and her continued friendship. I should also remember Laren Stover who effected our getting together in the first place.

If there is anyone I have left out, I apologize. My thanks go to everyone who helped make this book possible.

—J.M.
New York, 1989

Introduction

FROM *HAIR*
TO *HEAVEN*

*" Every one of them is the best possible
version of themselves imaginable. They live
in the heavens. They're like mythological
beings whom we fashion ourselves after in
moments of weakness."*

—Diane Keaton, on film stars in *Still Life*

She's been called the greatest actress in American film today, and the most reluctant star since Garbo. Everyone, to
some extent, knows Diane Keaton, either from having fallen in
love with her and the style she created in *Annie Hall*, or having
heard about her well-publicized affairs with Woody Allen and
Warren Beatty. But who is Diane Keaton?

She came to public attention as Woody's and Warren's girl,
but—more important—she's one of the greatest actresses on
screen today. The most accomplished comedienne since Carole
Lombard, Diane Keaton is also a dramatic actress of outstanding force, and a singer with a haunting voice. She has been a
Broadway star in both comedy and musical comedy, singing
and dancing onstage.

She has been on the cover of *Time* and *Newsweek*, the London
Sunday Times Magazine, *Vanity Fair*, *Rolling Stone*, and *Interview*,
to name just a few of the hundreds of magazines she's been
featured in around the world. She's been talked about, inter-

viewed, and analyzed. She's familiar to millions, but still she remains an enigma.

She thinks of herself in derogatory terms, yet she's considered one of the most beautiful women to appear on the silver screen since the young Katharine Hepburn. She, too, is a rebel, a fighter, and an icon in her way of dress.

If one person could be said to be the most influential woman of style of the latter seventies and the eighties it was Diane Keaton. Even during this decade, despite all the applause and accolades given to Nancy Reagan, H.R.H. Diana, the Princess of Wales, and all those aspiring society matrons who dress in Haute Couture, it is Keaton with her highly individual and unconventional mode of dress who has made such a style of multi-layered outfits, and has been a major fashion influence both here and in Europe.

Now, aged forty-three, she's at the height of her career. After twenty-one films, one Academy Award and a second nomination, two documentary films she conceived and directed, three Broadway shows, numerous nightclub acts, and two books, she's what they call in the business "a bankable asset." One of the highest-paid actresses in Hollywood, she can choose any film she wants.

First appearing in the quintessential musical of the sixties, *Hair*, she was noticed because she was the only one of the "tribe" not to take off her clothes in the then-shocking nude scene. Her modesty is legendary, yet given the right dramatic situation she will bare all, appearing nude in *Looking for Mr. Goodbar* in 1977. However, she will do it only if it is authentic for the role and the scene.

Ironically, it has been Keaton's personal life that has gained her so much attention: Her well-publicized affairs with Woody Allen and Warren Beatty have made headlines all over the world. Early on, as a rising star, she would talk about herself, even admitting that she was in analysis, but now she does not, especially about her private life: "I don't think people know what they're doing or what price they're going to have to pay for giving up so much of themselves to this vast audience of people who just take it and throw it out," she says. "And then you've given up something that means something to you, that should be private. It takes away from the specialness of it."

There are many qualities to Keaton, qualities that make her appeal so obvious in every interview she has done; her strength and her self-effacement, her loyalty, her work with old people, her wish for privacy, her knack for attracting attention, and perhaps most of all, her talent for showing the human frailty in the characters she portrays on screen.

If there is one common thread in all of the parts she has played, it is that in every one, even the period pieces, she has portrayed some aspect of what women feel today, what women are looking for, and what women fear. In her acting she exposes her vulnerability, and the audience identifies emotionally. Perhaps more than any other actress of the last twenty years she has shown in her roles what a tragic comedy life is.

She is real, and her truthfulness and honesty come through in her roles, which is why she appeals so much to us. Although a star, she is as far from the image of a star that one can imagine.

Keaton is no cardboard beauty, she is a woman who encapsulates what femininity is all about in today's America. Most of all she wants to be understood on her own terms and accepted for who *she* is as a person.

But trying to find that person is extremely difficult.

Her adamant and steadfast refusal to talk about herself has, naturally, made her even more fascinating to the media and the public, always avid for every last detail of their favorite stars' lives. It's simple human curiosity, of course, but Diane doesn't believe self-exposure is a necessary sacrifice for her to make. As she once said about actors' propensity to bare their souls to the public, "I hate reading confessional interviews with actors. Here's why. It's more than just an invasion of privacy. When I hear things people say on talk shows or read them in print, I think the basis of most of what they're saying is, 'Please like me. I had this or that problem, but please like me.'"

Diane's reticence to talk to the press or express herself in public is the most obvious indication of her contrary nature. She desperately wants to be loved and liked, not only on a personal level, which is vital to her, but also for her work, which is so necessary for her own self-evaluation. Privately, she knows that she *has* to give herself up to publicity, because it is a fact of life for a star, but she resents it for the intrusion it imposes on what she considers her private life, which, because of her status, isn't private at all. And, deep down inside, she must realize that her reticence makes her even more alluring to the public. It's a Catch-22 that Diane has not yet resolved. Because of her fierce protection of her personal life, writer Dominick Dunne, in a 1975 *Vanity Fair* article, compared her to Greta Garbo. And as they were with Garbo, people are all the more fascinated by Keaton, *because* of the mystery surrounding her.

But the reason for her reticence is not that of the aloof star who believes she is above it all, it is simply that she can't believe what all the fuss is about. "Movie stars aren't that important anymore. It's not such a big thing now. Rock stars are the real fascination. They've got more money and they're more decadent. Today's movie stars are just working people." Acting is her profession, her craft, and her art, and she believes that her performances should stand on their own. Yet, being a consummate technician, she sees what's wrong with each of them, and there are very few that she feels are good. As Woody Allen once put it, "Diane feels that what she is doing is not good enough because her standards are so high." It's indicative of her true modesty that when the author approached her about this biography, and asked if she would be willing to participate, she replied, "No. I don't know why you want to do it anyway, but if you want to do it, go ahead."

What Diane Keaton doesn't quite realize is how many people really admire her. And when one looks into her private life and realizes what she had to overcome to release her natural talent, it's all too easy to think of those sparkling eyes and wonderful smile and fall totally in love with her.

The secret to understanding Diane Keaton lies in all her roles because she has put so much of herself in all of them. Yet she isn't Linda or Kay or Luna or Sonja or Annie or Theresa or Renata or Louise Bryant or Faith or Mrs. Soffel; they are a composite portrait of her. While each of her roles has its own identity, they could not have been created without part of Diane in each one. They are women as diverse as anyone could find; they have their weaknesses and their triumphs, and how Diane could have found that essential part of herself to make them real demonstrates the extent of her acting ability.

Her charisma was evident right from the beginning, noticed by as an experienced a performer as Jack Benny, who, after seeing *Play It Again, Sam* on Broadway, told Woody, "That girl is going to be gigantic!" But, even so, it wasn't an easy rise to fame; Diane was out of work for years at a time, and was hardly noticed in her first couple of films. Although most people missed her in *The Godfather*, playing Al Pacino's wife, David Thomson in the prestigious publication *Sight and Sound* said of her performance as Kay Adams, "Her presence is alive with uncompromising kindness. She is capable of playing a decent person in any film committed to human values. The comparison I think of is with Ingrid Bergman in the Rossellini films."

Yet Diane had to wait five years to overcome her reputation as a rather vapid, though funny WASP who played in Woody Allen's movies and happened to be his girl. It says more about how convincing she was in the roles than the truth about her intelligence and talent.

With *Annie Hall* and *Looking for Mr. Goodbar*, Diane's real talent was recognized. Shortly thereafter, Richard Schickel, film critic of *Time* magazine, when asked to appraise her talent for the London *Sunday Times*, said, "She has to be the most interesting actress in the American cinema. She can make the definitive portrayal of the modern American woman. She's a quietly gritty girl, rather more subtle than people will allow. She'll find the shading in a part and get to the truth. I'm sure she's going to give us a lot of surprises."

Diane's ability to get to the truth was something her peers and directors had realized long before, but because of her ability to play comedy, she was considered a lightweight by the public. *Goodbar* and Woody's serious Bergman-like *Interiors* made it clear that she had range and force, and her performance in Warren Beatty's *Reds*, made under the most difficult conditions, earned her a second Oscar nomination.

Like Woody, Warren is most emphatic about Diane's talent: "She's constantly in search of something that's true. She has no interest in the delivery of a punch line; she cares only about the true situation, which then gives a wonderful dignity to a great joke writer like Woody. And in a film with political implications, she searches for what's true in a person and absolves the situation of being preachy or propagandistic. In other words, she has a built-in bullshit detector."

Diane's "bullshit detector" led her in the eighties to take on a variety of straight roles, from *Shoot the Moon* to *Crimes of the Heart*. More and more she was concerned with finding parts that were meaningful to her, from comedy to period pieces, from forceful domestic dramas to epics about global problems, but especially roles that concerned love and motherhood in all their variations. She was also looking for roles that would stretch her acting skills. She is as critical of herself as she is of others, telling *Newsweek* in 1982, "I'm a tough observer. I'm looking for anything that has any kind of life. If it's not the usual reaction, I don't care. If people act like jerks and they do something wrong, that's still better than being phony. I mean look at Vanessa Redgrave. When I'm looking at her and see her face fill up with feeling, that's coming from someplace that's even more than herself."

Obviously Diane Keaton sets the highest standards for herself and continues to feel that her work isn't good enough. Ten years ago Woody said, "She is always afraid she is never going to work again. She worries that she hasn't earned her success." To a certain extent Diane still feels that today, yet her performances in this decade have been some of the best in current cinema, and many of her peers believe she should have been nominated for an Academy Award for two of them. Sadly these films have not been great commercial successes, and it wasn't until 1987, when she came back to full-blown comedy in *Baby Boom*, that the public came back to see her for a box-office success.

Diane has been lucky in one respect. From the late seventies onwards Hollywood has been more concerned with good parts for women than ever before. Partially as a result of women's liberation, which has forced producers to consider these roles as salable, and partially because more women are working in responsible positions in film, we have been lucky enough to see the rise of such superb actresses as Ellen Burstyn, Glenn Close, Faye Dunaway, Sally Field, Jane Fonda, Jessica Lange, Vanessa Redgrave, Meryl Streep, Sissy Spacek, Kathleen Turner, Sigourney Weaver, and, of course, Diane, to name a few of the brilliant actresses Hollywood has at its disposal, along with the new crop of younger actresses coming up.

Certainly these performers have not had to fight for the right role as, say, Joan Crawford, Bette Davis, Susan Hayward, Katharine Hepburn, Carole Lombard, and Rosalind Russell did in their time. This Renaissance of great women's roles afforded Diane some wonderful parts, yet she still found it expedient to go out and search for vehicles that she believes in, which led her to take on the role of director and, eventually, producer.

The documentary *Heaven* was her ultimate attempt to communicate a message through the medium she knows so well: film. Unfortunately *Heaven* was not regarded highly, but it was a brave effort to question whether there is life after death or not. This is a concept that concerns all of us as we grow older, something we ponder in the deep recesses of our minds, whether we are religious or not.

Heaven demonstrates a philosophical side to Diane that isn't apparent from talking to her. Because of her reticence to discuss herself, Diane is said to be inarticulate. In the beginning of her career, before she started to read voraciously and inquire about a multitude of subjects in which she has since become knowledgeable, Diane was often at a loss for words. Now she uses her speech pattern as a clever defense mechanism to avoid answering questions, punctuating her sentences with many "Wows," "Oh, yeahs," "Umms," and "Hmms." But then, she is far more visually than verbally oriented. As an artist and an actress, feelings are just as important to her as words, and when one sees her reacting to something in a film you know that she doesn't need words—her expression tells it all.

This is one of the reasons that Diane has turned away from the stage and now concentrates almost exclusively on films. It is easier for her to express herself in the subtle way that a Panavision camera requires. It's difficult to analyze why some actors come across better on the screen than others, but all screen actors must come across for the camera.

It's not a question of projection, but simply that the camera has to love an actor. That was the secret of many of the great stars' success; think of James Dean and Marilyn Monroe. Diane has this quality, but with her it's more intangible: It's her ability to react. Woody Allen hit the nail on the head at the beginning of their collaboration, when she auditioned for *Play It Again, Sam*, saying that acting with Diane wasn't like acting, it was like having a conversation. She has the ability to listen.

Film requires a simpler truth than acting in the theater. The camera relentlessly demands reality, which is what Diane unerringly gives to the screen. As she gets older, Diane's search for the truth becomes more sharply honed. She is a far better actress now than the young California ingenue who bounced to fame in *Hair*, and the woman who made *Heaven* is a completely different person. She has gone through triumph and experienced sadness, and *all* of this can be seen in her current portrayals. She still has her doubts and insecurities of course; she's now worried about getting older and finding the right roles . . .

and finding love. But one thing we can be sure of is that the audience will benefit from Diane's personal search for "heaven."

As William Shakespeare said, in what is probably his best metaphor for life, "All the world's a stage, and all the men and women merely players; They have their exits and their entrances; And one man in his time plays many parts, his acts being seven stages." Diane has only played a few of the roles that are in her. Whether she goes on to concentrate on her acting, or decides to concentrate on directing and producing, or even feels she will be more stimulated expressing herself in her collages and photography, the sure bet is that we have only seen three or four of her "seven stages."

1

CALIFORNIA
GIRL

Diane Hall was born in Highland Park, Los Angeles, on January 5, 1946. Though only a short distance in terrestrial terms from Hollywood, her family was light years away from the glamour of the movie colony; they were "ordinary people," of the sort so well characterized by Steven Spielberg in his films set in California suburbia.

Her father, Jack Hall, comes from an Irish Catholic family that migrated to California from Nebraska when his mother (now immortalized as Grammy Hall) was a child. Diane's mother, Dorothy Keaton, is also a native Californian. Her parents are the same age, born in 1921, and typically American. There was nothing special or different about them except, perhaps, that when Diane was ten her mother won the "Mrs. Los Angeles" title, which is part of the "Mrs. America" beauty contest. Diane says of this occasion, "It was all like a dream sequence for me. They open the curtains. There's your mother. And then suddenly they call out your mother's name as the winner." She continues, "My mother's just wonderful. I never resented her. I was so proud of her. I call her every week."

When Diane was five the growing, close-knit family moved to Santa Ana when Jack was appointed engineer for Orange County. In those days that area was a far cry from what it is today. Diane wistfully remembers it as being full of orange groves, but the county was in fact booming and farming was rapidly being replaced by tract houses and K-Marts.

The family wasn't rich and didn't socialize much, so the children became self-reliant and resourceful. Diane was a born performer and quickly organized her younger siblings—two sisters, Dorrie (who looks very much like her) and Robin, and their brother, Randy, into an acting troupe, with herself writing, directing, and starring in the plays they performed on a stage constructed with curtains on the backyard patio. During the winter they improvised pantomimes in front of the living room fireplace. Costumes were devised from hand-me-downs and thrift-shop forays. Though these childhood dramatics began as fantasy and monster tales, very early on Diane graduated to dramas about domestic problems and child-parent relationships. What's amazing is that it sounds so like the Diane Keaton of today. The family's passion for amateur dramatics was such that her mother, Dorothy, says, "We never watched much TV because they were so much better."

The family favorite was her version of *Bonnie and Clyde* in which she played Clyde—the role acted by Warren Beatty in the film. Much later, Beatty sat entranced in the Hall home watching an 8-millimeter home movie version of Diane's *Bonnie and Clyde*. He found it hilarious and insisted on seeing it time and time again.

Fantasy played an important role in Diane's development. In an interview in 1987, thirty-two years after the fact, she stated, "I think nine was my favorite year. At that time I didn't want to be anything else but nine. I had seen *Peter Pan* and of course I wanted to be Peter Pan. I didn't want to be Wendy. Forget her—she's out. I wanted to be Peter Pan. And I didn't want to be ten. You know, the whole two-digit thing."

It's understandable that at this point in her life, with the uncertainty and fear children have about growing up, with all that it entails, that she found a certain comfort in religion. "I was always pretty religious as a kid, but I had trouble with Jesus early on because I couldn't understand that there was a son of God here on earth. I was primarily interested in religion because I wanted to go to heaven."

Now, however, Diane doesn't consider religion to be a vital force in her life. "We were Methodists, but that went the way of the wind. It was an influence on me in some ways, but not the main one." Perhaps it is telling that for this introspective, insecure young girl, much of her childhood fervor was spent, not in asking for things, as most people do, but in apologizing. "I used to pray a lot. You know, apologize."

None of this is to say that she was unhappy as a child. It's obvious that the opposite was true, and ironically it was through the church that she discovered what was to be her role in life. She joined the church choir and discovered singing, and through that acting. In fact, for most of her formative years her ambition was to become a singer and musical comedy actress.

There's no doubt that Diane felt deeply insecure and hid her shyness by creating an extravagant persona. While on the outside she was an extrovert, embarrassing the family by imitating Charlie Chaplin or mimicking old ladies in a loud voice in supermarkets and stores, inside she was most likely a loner—one who preferred to go outside and sing alone in the moonlight.

"Communication with higher nature is what it was," says Keaton now, with a grin. She told Joan Juliet Buck in the March 1978 cover story of *Vanity Fair* that she was fascinated by rocks and stones as a child. "Those little boxes from Knott's Berry Farm or Disneyland with crystals inside them—to me that was the most beautiful thing to own. When you're a kid you fantasize about gems. Beauty seems to be diamonds and rubies and emeralds. The Emerald City in *The Wizard of Oz* was very important—the most beautiful place that ever was, all green crystals." Certainly this is someone whose recollections of childhood are those of wishing to escape the harshness of reality.

Partially this was because she never felt herself beautiful or talented. Even though she was instinctively drawn to performing, her insecurities overwhelmed her. When she was six, for instance, she started to cry during a church recitation, and her mother had to come and carry her off the stage. Perfectly natural for a child of that age, but in reminiscing about her experience her reaction isn't the shame, but the fact that the audience applauded her! While on one level she denigrated herself, on another, deeper, level she was beginning to come to the realization that there was a spark of talent within her, and she was beginning to criticize herself.

Yet her self-criticism never stopped her from trying. In school most of her efforts went into the choir and trying out for the talent contest. Her personal appraisal of her own worth is seen as early as the ninth grade. In a school Christmas talent contest she chose to parody herself by blacking out two teeth and singing, with another student, "All I Want for Christmas Is My Two Front Teeth." Like any clown, comedian, or comedienne, there is pathos behind the funny performance; in Diane's case it was born out of insecurity, and it started early. What she didn't realize then was that these insecurities would make her one of the best comedy actresses of her time and give her the range to become equally brilliant as a serious actress.

Looking at pictures now of Diane growing up, it's difficult to understand why she held herself in such low esteem. At three she was a chubby little girl, but adorable; by the time she was eleven her face, while very round, was beginning to show the Keaton hallmarks—large, almond-shaped eyes and a turned-up nose with a bump on the end; by fourteen the cheekbones were becoming prominent and she had grown into her ears. Admittedly it wasn't until she was eighteen that the real beauty she is became more apparent, but in every picture of her until then there was always that wonderful smile.

Academically she was a poor student. The highest score she ever received in school was for interpreting the meaning of photographs in an "Abstract Reasoning" test. And even then she had to go home and ask her mother what abstract reasoning meant. ("So I'd know what I was good at," she says now!) In later years she has always maintained that she learned nothing at school; she was drawn only to the arts. Apart from singing she loved art and can still remember a collage she created at high school that filled a whole wall. It was made up of black and white photographs and varnished with an orange-toned shellac. "I thought it was very, profoundly beautiful." Her visual sensitivity and artistic creativity is a gift she remains very involved with to this day. With the three R's, though, she felt totally lost. As she told the London *Sunday Times*, "School? I went to school as a social occasion—it was nothing more than that. I was more interested than anything to be in the choir and the talent show. I was always motivated in performing. I was shy and didn't have a lot of friends. I really didn't have an education—I was a bad student. I compensated with personality!" She added, in her characteristically self-denigrating way, "I don't think that has helped much, either."

For the most part, therefore, Diane spent her time and energy in singing in the girls' choir, the Debutantes, and trying out for the school theatrical productions. She had already learned that being behind the footlights was a warm, safe place to be.

On a more personal level, things were much harder for her. In her adolescent fantasies, like most teenagers, she dreamed of dating the school jocks. She was always falling in love with the too-good-to-be-true California boys on the basketball team— "Because they were unattainable. I wasn't up for the real stuff"—but inevitably ended up with the amiable nerds. In trying to conform she did try out for cheerleading, but that didn't work: "I didn't quite make it into that popular mode." Instead Diane turned herself into an unconventional fashion statement, wearing shorter skirts and teasing her hair higher than anyone else, breaking the school rules on dress—"White lipstick and black stockings. Oh, wow." Her mother later recalled in a *New York Post* article, "Diane had an absolute panic to be different. She wore black stockings and eye makeup as black as her stockings." And a school friend Leslie Morgan remembers, "We were the high school wierdos. We thought of ourselves as two beatnicks, but even then Diane had a great sense of style—her mother made lots of her dresses."

Already Diane was using her individuality to create a persona. As her sister Dorrie says about this stage of her development, "Everything she did was always big. Her laugh was big. She walked like a truck driver. She exaggerated everything." It's no wonder that she was voted "Miss Personality" in her senior year. In that same year she played the second lead in the school production of *Little Mary Sunshine*. Although she puts herself down by saying, "The star was beautiful; I was the funny one," she made an impression on the audience. "I sang my solo and then I was backstage, and I heard this sound. And then I couldn't believe it. It was applause, and they were clapping for me, and it was *so loud!*" While she claims in an interview that she was terrible in this production, she went on to Santa Ana College, where she concentrated on her first love, singing, and drama.

She made her debut there in the musical *Bye Bye Birdie*, and again, of this performance she says she was terrible, and that her teacher suggested she was wasting her time acting. Bob Blaustone of the Santa Ana Theater Department has a different recollection however. "We recognized her acting talent straight away. She was terrific onstage and showed her abilities early on. In real life she couldn't express herself at all, she was next to incoherent." Blaustone cast her in *Carousel*, and she spent two summers at the school's summer stock program in Mancos, Colorado, under Lee Ford. After a year Diane dropped out of Santa Ana, and enrolled in Orange Coast College. There, Diane came under the tutelage of Lucien Scott, who was to have a great impact on her career. She did more work in musicals, appearing in the Orange Coast College production of Rodgers and Hammerstein's *The Sound of Music*. But for some reason, she dropped out after only a few months.

Basically, Diane's childhood was over. A childhood she has described as being typical of California—"The beach, you know." Though in fact, the beach wasn't as important to her as most California kids. While she went water-skiing, scuba diving, and surfing with her father, she disliked the way she looked in a swimsuit. "I've always had a little bit of trouble about swimming gear. I totally loathe and despise it. I have definite opinions about my body."

Yet, while not fitting in, it was a childhood that she loved. In a recent interview, she said that she never really wanted to grow up, but she had. It was time for her to leave the nest, the warm, totally supportive, close-knit family where she could feel secure and not have to worry about her goal of "being liked."

Within the loving environment of her family she could be natural. While she considers both her father and mother as somewhat strict, even describing Dorothy as "American Gothic," the love and pride she feels for them is always there. One can sense it in the way she describes her father's strength and her mother's devotion. They in their wisdom decided it would be good for Diane to go out on her own after she had dropped out of college. Diane had a very poor scholastic record and seemingly little ambition apart from her singing. She had to decide what she wanted to do with her life, and her wise parents obviously felt she couldn't do it living at home.

Up to now the family had always vacationed together, taking camping trips into the Southern California desert and visiting Tijuana, and even, the year before, driving across the country to go to the New York World's Fair. (This trip was a kind of family graduation present; Diane had graduated from high school, and Dorothy had earned her degree at college, which she'd gone back to when she was forty.)

This time Diane went much further; to Europe, where she

spent most of her time there staying with a family on a USAF base at Karlsrule in West Germany. When she came back she had decided what she wanted to do.

She *knew* she wanted to sing and act. "It was [always] easier for me to do things in front of people than for me to be socially integrated. I'm not—I'm still not—a socially integrated person. I wish I were. I think I would have had a better life if I were." She was encouraged in her ambition by the whole family, especially her feisty grandmother, Mary Hall.

2

L.A. TO BROADWAY

Diane's drama teacher from Orange Coast College, Lucien Scott, suggested that Diane go to New York to pursue her acting. He felt that Sanford Meisner, at his Neighborhood Playhouse School of the Theater, would be the best person to develop her untrained talent, so Diane applied to audition for the theater school. This would take money, but the Halls were more affluent now. Jack had resigned from the county job to start his own civil engineering company and had invested wisely in real estate in booming Orange County. Her parents were willing to support Diane in her chosen vocation.

It was a big step for them to take; their first child would be living three thousand miles away, alone, in an unknown city. So Jack and Dorothy, not knowing anything about the theater but with that stubborn individualism that they had instilled in their children, decided to investigate for themselves. They bundled the four kids into a Ford van and drove to New York, as they had done to visit the World's Fair the year before. The Neighborhood Playhouse on East 54th Street in Manhattan passed this vetting, and Diane passed her audition. Not only was she accepted, but she also won a scholarship. Obviously the junior college teacher who had advised her to quit acting was in the minority!

It was a difficult decision for Diane to make. She did want to study acting, but she was still the same insecure girl inside who didn't want to leave home. However the determination of the Halls overcame her fears, and she decided to go. "Sometimes one knows how strong the impulse to *do* is," she says, adding, "I didn't know how really strong until a lot afterward."

Happily, Diane loved the school and blossomed under Meisner's tutelage. "That is where I got the first feeling about what acting could really be," says Keaton. "Sandy forced you to pay attention to what other people are doing and let it affect you. It sounds like nothing, but it's not easy. You know what you want when you do a scene. But what I learned was never to take for granted what the other person is going to do, and if they give you something unusual, go with that."

She also says, "He gave me a way of approach which was natural and, I think, alive. And very simple too." (The extent of Meisner's influence on her can be inferred from the fact that this is a perfect description of Diane Keaton's brilliance as an actress, and the secret to the depth and reality of her portrayals.)

Naturally she kept up with her first love, singing. She even joined a rock band, The Road Runners, formed by Guy and Pip Gillette, whom she accompanied singing, dancing and playing the tambourine. Diane says that she was "real bad," but she loved it singing Aretha Franklin songs and "In the Midnight Hour." The Road Runners used to do gigs in the environs of New York, and got paid ten dollars a time!

Diane also studied dance with the legendary Martha Graham. Graham's teaching doesn't seem to have helped her walk however. She still stomps around, looking "as if she's leading a Girl-Scout troop" as writer David Edelstein ungallantly, but perceptively, describes it. But there's no doubt that her deportment did improve from her dance lessons.

On graduating from the Neighborhood Playhouse, Diane

Hall got her first professional job acting, singing, and dancing in a summer stock production of the British musical, *Oh! What a Lovely War*. Like every other actor, she had to join Equity, the actors' union, which already had a Diane Hall on their books. Equity doesn't allow any two actors to register under the same name, so Diane Hall had to change hers. She took her mother's maiden name, Keaton, and her sister's name, Dorrie. "After six months it dawned on me how terrible I was . . . after all, Dorrie was *her* name . . . she *is* Dorrie Hall . . . I think I did it because I like her, and thought her good qualities would rub off on me, but if I was a flop as an actress, all the bad reviews would be going to *her*." But "Dorrie Keaton" was how Diane was billed for this production in the small theater in Woodstock in upstate New York. She was elated and had visions of herself as a Broadway star of musical comedy—"Gee, I'm glad I wasn't!"

Unfortunately when the summer season was finished the aspiring actress, like ninety percent of the actors on Equity's lists, couldn't find work. After several months of going to auditions and trying out for parts, the despondent and rejected twenty-one-year-old actress decided to give it up. She went back to California seeking refuge and security with her family.

This was the only time in Diane Keaton's twenty-year career that she faltered, even though there were some hard times ahead. Recently, she gave *Interview* magazine an insight into what she was feeling at this point. She wasn't sure whether she really wanted to pursue acting. "I remained vague about everything, I think. I couldn't face the fact that I really wanted to do it. If I did admit I wanted to act, I would be cursed. It was kind of a Catholic thing—a superstitious way of thinking. I thought I'd better not admit to myself that I wanted to be an actress, because then it couldn't come true. All this, of course, is crazy." Mary (Grammy) Hall, her tough, no-nonsense, Irish grandmother soon put a stop to that. Diane was sent back to New York with her determination, ambition, and confidence renewed, as well as with her parents' continued financial support.

It was now early 1968, and soon after she returned to New York, now calling herself Diane Keaton, she auditioned for a part in a small Off-Broadway rock musical show that had made its debut at Joseph Papp's Public Theater in Greenwich Village, transferred to the Cheetah, and was now on its way to Broadway. Although she had experience with rock music from her time with The Road Runners, she was again rejected.

"I went out to the elevator, and man, did I feel bad. I mean, I felt bad. I was thinking, 'This is ridiculous.'" Luckily one of the producers, who was French—probably executive producer, Bertrand Castelli—caught up with her before she got into the elevator and said, "No, you stay." Keaton still doesn't know why he decided to keep her when director Tom O'Horgan, producer Michael Butler, and, presumably, writers James Rado and Gerome Ragni (who appeared in the show as Claude and Berger, respectively), as well as composer Galt MacDermot, thought her resumé and photographs were less than adequate and were not impressed by her audition. This show was a rock musical protesting against the social values of the day and the war in Vietnam: The name of the show was *Hair*.

So Diane became a member of the "tribe," with the part of "Parent." (Actually the tribe was the chorus in the show, but the media used the nomenclature inclusively.) "I didn't know it was going to be a Broadway hit," she later told George Perry of the London *Sunday Times*. "It really was a strange atmosphere. A lot of people in the show weren't professionals, but became professionals immediately. All that peace and love—they were as competitive as hell!"

In her naïveté Diane didn't realize what had happened to her. She recalls that the biggest thought on her mind when she was in *Hair* was wondering how long it would last and therefore how long she could stay in New York before having to go back to California! Even the hype surrounding the show, which had moved to Broadway, didn't seem to affect her. "I think I was pretty isolated. I had no sense of the world. I did not hang out. I didn't want to."

Meanwhile *Hair* had become a media event. The tribe was interviewed on television, photographed for *Vogue* by Richard Avedon, and taken up by what Diane calls "the *Women's Wear Daily* set." The cast became famous for "half a minute." (The quotes are Keaton's. Notice that she sarcastically reduces herself and the cast to less significance in this play on Andy Warhol's famous remark about everyone being famous for fifteen minutes.)

"I remember getting invited, with the rest of the 'tribe,' as the cast was called, to Fire Island. We were put up by some very rich people because we were so *cute*. We were very in," Keaton recalls. But, just like her school days in Santa Ana, she didn't exactly fit in. "I was never a true member of the tribe, although I did like the show." Much of this could have been due to her introspection, she didn't realize what an impact she had made: An impact that was a direct result of her shyness. She achieved instant notoriety as the only member of the cast *not* to take her clothes off. In a musical "that wasn't much for individual performances," she had made her mark.

Even in the Swinging Sixties, it's possible that Diane, very naïve and unsure of herself, was still a virgin. Whether that was the reason, or that she hated her body, she would not expose herself to the vulgar gaze of the public, despite the peer pressure that she must have been under from the rest of the cast. "It wasn't for psychological reasons," she said later, "it was just that I was very scared." The famous nude scene in *Hair* was optional for the cast, and only two or three participated in the beginning. Then more and more of the cast began to strip, possibly because they were paid an extra fifty dollars to do it. Diane felt so strongly about it she was never able to take advantage of this extra money.

Needless to say, the experience onstage did begin to awaken her sensuality and sexuality. She now admits to peeking at the other cast members when *they* stripped down onstage! "I was quite curious," she later confessed to *Time* magazine, continuing, with one of her huge grins, "yeah. I mean, I wouldn't say I was *not* curious, you know. I took a look or two, sure."

Hair opened at the Biltmore Theater on West 47th Street on April 29, 1968. Six months after the Broadway opening, the star of the show, Lynn Kellogg, left. Diane was her understudy, and took over for a week. Michael Butler, the producer, decided she was good enough to permanently take over the role of Sheila . . . on one condition.

"You can have the part if you lose weight and start trying to be a little more attractive." Keaton still had some of her baby fat, and was not making the best of herself; even then, she didn't realize her potential and accept how beautiful she really was. Butler put her on a special diet that involved getting a shot every day which was distilled from the placenta of an unborn lamb. For the treatment, the company paid half and Diane paid half, for thirty-five dollars a week. Diane lost her excess weight and came down to the 115 pounds she remains at today.

Her name was up in lights on Broadway! But being Diane, she couldn't really believe what she had achieved.

"I was living alone on the West Side, in a one-room apartment with the bathroom out in the hallway and the bathtub in the kitchen, right? I didn't feel like I had arrived with *Hair*." But she *had* arrived.

Diane didn't stay long with the tribe. Certainly she didn't want to be identified and cast as a pseudo-hippy actress whose sole claim to fame was that she wouldn't strip onstage, which at the time was about all she had going for her.

A new comedy, which the theater world was excited about, was being cast, and Diane auditioned for it. Keaton myth has it that she heard about the auditions and simply asked herself along. Not true. There was a definite campaign by those who believed she was right for the part. Before the end of the year, Lucien Scott, who had advised her to study with Sanford Meisner at the Neighborhood Playhouse, recommended her to another of his former students, Joe Hardy, who was about to

direct the second play of one of the most brilliant comic performers and writers in the country. Keaton landed a starring
role in *Play It Again, Sam*.

In 1968, the general public was not as aware of Woody Allen
as they are now, but he had already written and acted in one of
the most successful films of the decade, *What's New, Pussycat?*,
redubbed a dreadful Japanese C-movie and transformed it into
the hilarious *What's Up, Tiger Lily?*, and his first Broadway play,
Don't Drink the Water, had just completed a highly successful
598-performance run at the Morosco Theater.

Diane was to play the role of Linda Christie, the wife of Dick
Christie (Anthony Roberts, who was so successful in Allen's
first play), who is the best friend of Allan Felix, the central
character. Felix is hung up on the film *Casablanca*, and it is in his
West Village apartment that the action takes place. The role was
played by Allen in his Broadway debut.

Was it just another audition for Diane? That's doubtful. Certainly she had shown a penchant for comedy as a neophyte in
her school productions, but that was not exactly the sort of experience that a top producer like David Merrick was looking for.
She knew that in order to succeed she had to extend her range
(where is the rest of the cast of *Hair* today?), and that this part
could be a breakthrough for her. Whatever rhyme or reason led
the aspiring young actress to take the chance, fate must also
have played a role. She not only got the part, she also met, and
became involved with, one of the comic geniuses of our time.
The meeting was to change her life.

3

WOODY

The first time Diane meets Allen Stewart Konigsberg is almost Allenesque in its layers of comedy, insecurity, and intensity. One has to imagine a darkened theater decked out for auditions with that one glaring, unshielded light bulb over the stage.

Picture, if you can, an extremely nervous, very short, thirty-two-year-old writer and comic with more insecurities than the whole of the Federal Government in Washington, D.C., put together, nervously waiting for the appearance of yet another young actress who must be exactly right to balance the love triangle in his creation, *Play It Again, Sam*, a brilliant if somewhat loony tribute to the classic film *Casablanca*.

Everything Konigsberg has heard about her can only increase his nervousness. She's too tall, she's the star of *the* hot musical on Broadway, *Hair*, she's beautiful, she can sing, act, and dance, and she's the ultimate WASP from California, the antithesis of his own Jewish upbringing in Brooklyn.

And in walks Diane: equally unsure, probably more nervous than Konigsberg with the knowledge that she hasn't had much experience on the stage, certainly not in comedy, and that she

will have to read with the playwright! She, who never got a
good grade in anything as difficult as English composition. He
is everything she would like to be—witty, erudite, brilliant, and
successful. Not handsome perhaps—but even so he could mean
the difference between failure and success in her career. This
audition is important to her, and she knows it.

Diane has always dressed differently, and most likely, she's
dressed even more originally than usual for this audition. One
can imagine, therefore, her fear when the author leaves the
anonymous back reaches of the auditorium and comes up
onstage, only to walk around and around her, without saying a
word. Then he asks her to take off her shoes!

Don't they like the way she looks, or is it, she wonders, just
to see if she will take her clothes off? With a sigh of relief she
realizes that this isn't a casting couch situation, it's simply a
foible of the playwright, who seems to be equally nervous, and
who wants to know how tall she is. After all, he's short, and,
worst of all, she's tall!

Without her shoes, Keaton, who is all legs, looks less tall,
and, better than that, in her stocking feet is only 5' 7", a scant
three-quarters of an inch taller than Allen. (He sees her as about
the same size.) She has passed the first test.

But can she act? Can she play comedy?

Sandy Meisner had already told producer David Merrick that
Diane was "the best young actress around," which was definitely in her favor, but Allen, as well as Joe Hardy, the director, would have to like her, too.

Allen recalls, "I thought she was great the second I saw her."
Not only did he find her beautiful, but he was more than comfortable with her natural acting style. "It wasn't like an actress
acting back, it was like we were really relating." She wasn't the
Broadway star that he, seeing himself as a lowly standup comic,
was dreading she would be.

For Diane's part, he wasn't the wordy intellectual who she
had been scared would consider her inadequate. "He was about

as tentative as I was. He seemed to be auditioning more than me, and it was his play. He was great!"

During rehearsals, despite playing lovers onstage, they remained colleagues only. "Outside of rehearsal I was frightened to talk to her, and she was frightened to talk to me and we'd go home separately every night and nothing ever happened," says Allen ruefully. However, on the pre-Broadway tour they were naturally thrown into each other's company. "We'd hang around together, nothing big, have dinner," recalls Allen. But Woody was beginning to become mesmerized by Diane. "Tony [Roberts] and I couldn't stop laughing at Diane. It was nothing you could quote later; she couldn't tell a joke if her life depended on it. Tony figured it out one time, what it is she does. He says she has this uncanny ability to project you back into an infantile atmosphere, and you 're suddenly a little kid again. There is something utterly guileless about her."

Whatever her quality was, it was intriguing and attractive to Woody, but it wasn't until they got to Washington that he finally got up the courage to ask her out alone. One thing led to another and they became lovers. "Maybe it was the Freudian lifting of inhibitions or something," he later told *Newsweek*. "You know, being in a different city from the one where my mother lived." In this statement Woody is probably being far less straightforward and confessional than he usually is in his writing and films. It was more likely that it wasn't his mother whom he was afraid of but his second wife, Louise Lasser (the actress television audiences came to love as Mary Hartman), whom he would divorce that year. (Although some sources say that Allen was married to Lasser until 1971.)

Whether Diane was the cause of the divorce or simply symptomatic of the problems between Allen and Lasser is a moot point. It's doubtful in light of the fact that Allen and Lasser must have come to an amicable arrangement regarding their differences, as Allen was to star her in a film he would make in 1971, *Bananas*, just as he had used her the previous year in *Take the Money and Run*. Whatever the truth of Woody's domestic situation in 1969, it was still a big jump for the shy young woman who wouldn't take her clothes off in the quintessential show about sex, drugs, and rock 'n' roll, to leap into the bed of a married man and actually move in with him. They started living together at the start of the Broadway run of *Play It Again, Sam*, which opened at the Broadhurst Theater on February 12, 1969.

It must have been a very special passion for someone as romantic as Diane to move in with a man eleven years older, and who was on the point of getting his second divorce. She must have been aware of censure, perhaps not from her family, but certainly from her peers. The theater world is a hotbed of gossip, and there were no doubt many snide remarks about the twenty-three-year-old actress getting the part by sleeping with the star.

What the Hall family thought of the liaison has never been voiced, though they have always said how much they liked Woody. Mind you, Mary Hall devoted quite a lot of time during the seventies, when she was over eighty, trying to fix Diane up with "nice young men" from her neighborhood, and the famous dinner scene from *Annie Hall* where Alvy (Allen) imagines Grammy Hall seeing him with a yarmulke, full beard, earlocks, and frock coat, while exaggerated, more than hints at Woody's perception of the family reaction.

Why then did these two seemingly disparate people fall for each other, thereby creating one of the most celebrated love stories in movie history?

One only has to examine their characters to see that under the surface they were ideally suited.

Allen (or Alan, depending on the source) Stewart Konigsberg was born on December 1, 1935, in the Flatbush section of Brooklyn, New York. For most of his schooldays he was semi-literate, preferring to spend his days playing baseball and basketball rather than studying. The only reading he ever did was looking at comic books, such as *Superman*, *Batman*, and *Mickey*

Mouse. It's doubtful that his parents, Martin and Nettie Konigsberg ever understood him; actually they hardly ever saw him. He spent nearly all his time on the streets playing ball, only coming back home to eat a tuna fish sandwich by himself at lunchtime, and returning for dinner. He even ate dinner alone. "I never ate dinner with my family," he told *Newsweek*. "I'd eat in the cellar or my bedroom, read my comic books, lock myself in my room and practice the clarinet and my card and coin tricks. It would drive my mother crazy."

It is easy to see why the young Allen was teased mercilessly at school. Even then he was rather short, certainly no "King's Mountain" (the literal translation of "Konigsberg") and they even laughed at his first two names, so he took to calling himself Frank. But still they laughed. He was no cowering wimp, however. From the age of eleven he was an avid New York Giants fan, which didn't exactly endear him to the other kids who were Brooklyn Dodger fans and understandably somewhat hostile!

Strangely enough, though Allen didn't read, he was a natural writer and there wasn't a week when his composition wasn't the one read out loud in class. After he was fifteen he began to take an interest in reading "only when I started going out with women who were more cultured and made demands on me that I felt I had to read to keep my end of the conversation up." While he wasn't into Kafka, Kierkegaard, Jung, Freud, Nietzsche, or even the Russian writers and philosophers he so likes to quote now, he wasn't boasting when he was talking about women. Woody married his first wife, Harlene Rosen, when they were both still teenagers. The marriage lasted five years.

Apart from baseball, young Allen got most of his education from show business. He naturally gravitated to the Flatbush Theater and saw every vaudeville show and movie that was presented there, writing down jokes on torn-up Raisinets boxes.

For most of his childhood he was a loner, undoubtedly suffering from an inferiority complex. Consistently depressed and fearful of death, Allen learned to overcome his neuroses with comedy. His perception of his childhood and his inadequacies is now central to his humor. "I was in analysis for years because of a traumatic childhood. I was breast fed through falsies," is just one example.

Allen's loneliness was definitely profound, but he began to find solace in music. He taught himself to play the clarinet and soprano saxophone simply by accompanying records. But like Keaton, academia was not for him and he was expelled from not one, but two, colleges, New York University and the City College of New York.

Nettie and Martin Konigsberg naturally didn't understand the prodigy they had brought forth, and were very hurt by his college performance. "My mother was a sensitive woman. When I was thrown out of college she locked herself in the bathroom and took an overdose of Mah-Jongg tiles."

One-liners like this were to start Allen Konigsberg on his career. While still at school he was selling jokes to press agents for twenty-five dollars a week, which he found far easier than working at a trade for the minimum wage of seventy-five cents an hour. "I'd give them fifty jokes a day. There was nothing to it. I'd get out of school, get on the BMT subway and start listing jokes. Always five to a page, ten pages." The jokes that poured from Allen's pen were used by columnists such as Earl Wilson.

Allen was soon writing material for comedians like Herb Shriner and Peter Lind Hayes, and his gags were so good that he attracted the attention of the producers of the most successful TV comedy show of the fifties. Still in his teens, Allen was asked to write for "Your Show of Shows," starring Sid Caesar. In this environment he could only progress, meeting and collaborating with such skilled writers as Mel Brooks, Danny Simon (Neil's brother), and Larry Gelbart. However the twenty-year-old, now "Woody" Allen, found them a little intimidating at first.

"I was much less extroverted than they were, and the emotional adjustment was very hard for me." He found it difficult to compete with them while they were fighting each other to get their lines on the show, yet they were all very helpful to him. He ended his apprenticeship writing for *The Garry Moore Show*, which he quit when he was ready to go on to the next stage of his career.

Woody's agents, Charles Joffe and Jack Rollins, persuaded him it was time to strike out on his own in stand-up comedy. He honed his act in Greenwich Village clubs and soon began to get bookings at famous clubs like New York's Bitter End and the Blue Angel as well as performing across the country. Television appearances followed and by the early sixties he had made his name and was recognized as one of the great comedic talents in the country. His records sold, his writing was appearing in that bastion of literacy *The New Yorker*, and then film producer Charles Feldman, after catching his show one night, asked him to write his first screenplay. Though Allen has later said he hated what they did with his script, *What's New, Pussycat?*, released in 1965, became the highest grossing comedy up to that time. It starred Peter Sellers and Peter O'Toole, and featured Woody Allen.

The next year, 1966, was very busy for Allen. Not only did his first play, *Don't Drink The Water*, open on Broadway, but he got married for the second time and found the time to acquire the rights to a schlocky Japanese secret agent film, which he transformed into the cockeyed *What's Up, Tiger Lily?*, later to become a cult film. Allen was then asked to play one of the most coveted roles in Hollywood, another secret agent—James Bond, 007. Woody played Bond in *Casino Royale* (along with a lot of other people, including David Niven and Orson Welles!).

Woody's next big venture was a screenplay he co-wrote with Mickey Rose called, *Take the Money and Run*, which he was eager for Jerry Lewis to direct. When that idea fell through, Joffe and Rollins, knowing his disappointment with the final version of *Pussycat*, suggested he direct the new film himself. They got $1.6 million from Palomar, who had financed *Pussycat*. It would mark the start of Rollins and Joffe's long relationship with Woody as his producers, as well as managers.

The story of an inept criminal, Virgil Starkwell (Allen), *Take the Money and Run* was shot in the style of a documentary montage which turns into narrative fiction. While not totally successful, and more in the vein of a Buster Keaton-Keystone Cops chase, the film has some great gags. It's worth noting that Allen took some directorial risks in this his first directing/writing/acting screen endeavor. Woody's new wife, Louise, co-starred with him.

Returning to Broadway for his next venture, *Play It Again, Sam*, Woody was already highly successful when he met Diane Keaton. But insecure as the struggling young actress was, so was he. About this he has been quoted as saying, "She was a Broadway star, and who was I? A cabaret comedian who had never been on the stage before." A typical Allenesque self-effacement, perhaps.

Diane was fresh, young, totally unmanipulative, and completely honest. "She came out of the boondocks of Southern California, completely guileless. She sees directly to the reality of a thing," he says, and one can understand his attraction to this sort of naïveté, especially in someone who could make him laugh. There is also the fact that Woody was suddenly thrust into the position of mentor with Diane. She was far less educated than he and he could teach her the things he had grown to admire and respect through his own self-education—the philosophers, thinkers, and writers he so loves to quote or parody, as well as his vast knowledge of theater and film. Their relationship was a tremendous boost to his fragile ego.

For Diane, though Woody was the pivotal figure in her life, it was far more of a partnership than a Svengalian relationship. Although he was her mentor and lover, she was a strong enough person that he was inspired, and, it must be said, intimidated by her. What Diane gave Woody was her innate visual sense.

"She has an utterly spectacular visual sense. I see many things today through her eyes, textures and forms I would never have seen without her. She showed me the beauty of the faces of old people. I'd never been sensitive to that before. And there's a certain warmth and poignance associated with young women I would never have seen without her. She's increased my affection for women in general." It's quite an admission for any man to make, and shows the depth of Woody's affection and appreciation for Diane.

The visual perception that she gave him has helped his career in no uncertain terms. These are the exact qualities that mark the maturing of Allen's style as a director; qualities that were not evident in the early films.

Under Woody's genius and tutelage Diane grew from a California ingenue into a sophisticated New York-based actress. When she met him she was lacking in formal education. Allen taught her about culture, the arts, and life, and gave her the encouragement to become the knowledgeable, thinking woman she is today.

What's fascinating is that he didn't use her talents until after their affair was ended. The film version of *Play It Again, Sam* wasn't made until 1972, and he didn't direct Diane until *Sleeper* in 1973. In fact, the next film Woody made, *Bananas*, starred Louise Lasser.

Most accounts suggest that Woody and Diane were together for years, even up to *Annie Hall*, which was made in 1976, but this is denied by Allen. In Lee Guthrie's biography of Woody he categorically states that he and Diane lived together only during the run of *Sam*, which closed on Broadway on March 14, 1970. Sometime around then Diane moved to her own apartment on East 68th Street. Their relationship wasn't terminated by the move; it was simply that they needed space apart. "It might be nice, we thought, to try it with her *not* living here. That was a mutual decision. And if we didn't like it, we'd move back in together . . . I mean. We were still lovers intermittently after that for a while. Gradually we sort of cooled down and drifted apart more." Allen maintains that although he loved her very deeply, neither of them was mature enough then to commit to a lasting relationship. And there was still the question of whether he was married to Miss Lasser or not, which would have put somewhat of a damper on any plans of marriage, if indeed they'd ever been close to making that decision.

What they did have, however, was an appreciation of each other that brought out their best and enabled both to overcome a few of their insecurities. Woody had introduced Diane to analysis, which he had been in since his early twenties, and this examination of herself, which lasted seven years, did a lot to help her. Judging by some of the scenes in *Annie Hall*, this mutual appreciation was rooted in their ability to laugh at their own and each other's insecurities and foibles.

Diane, normally completely tight-lipped about her private life, does go so far as to admit that "amusing things" did happen when they were in bed together. Another situation that must have made them laugh was when Diane finally persuaded Woody to take dance lessons, with her old teacher, Martha Graham, in 1973. As Woody says, rather apologetically, "Like most men who've tried a dance class, it was interesting but it wasn't fun. It's quite embarrassing for a thirty-eight-year-old person to buy a dance belt and leotards and sit in class. I didn't mind being there, but once you had to get up and prance across the floor with others and do the big, open steps, I couldn't make it. My sense of shame just overtook me."

Woody loved Diane's sense of humor, although he may have been slightly annoyed at her laughter when he described himself in tights. He sees her as an "honorary Jew." This is partially because the not-widely-read Diane tended to get things mixed up and once asked him if he was going to his parents' house for Yammacher Schlemmer—confusing the New York store with the Jewish high holy day.

He introduced her to many of the special delights New York had to offer, and experiencing that city of cities through his peculiar sense of life must have been illuminating. At the same time she was opening his eyes to things he had never seen, images she later showed in her photography books. There was also Diane's gusto for life, something the rather frail Woody had never experienced.

"She had the largest appetite of anyone I've ever known," he says. "After a ball game or a fight I'd take her to Frankie and Johnnie's and she'd have a steak and potatoes and marble cheesecake. Then we'd come home and she'd go into the kitchen and turn on a TV movie. She's always cold, so she'd turn on the stove, take her paintings out and put them on the kitchen table. And Bette Davis would be on and the stove would be wide open and she just had a steak dinner and she'd go to the freezer and take out frozen waffles and she'd start making them and have three or four of those. And I'd go into the kitchen later and find her frying up tacos. I couldn't believe it—I was awestruck by her appetite."

This quote from *Newsweek* suggests that they did live together on and off after *Sam*, as it would have been difficult for them to get to a ball game during the run of the show. Obviously Diane's moving into her own apartment was her way of finding independence. Remember, it was a period in which she was growing, not just as an actress, but as a woman, and she needed to explore life on her own, just as the solitary Woody needed to be by himself. Out of the love affair grew the most lasting and respectful friendship, which has not only made her career, but also helped his.

Probably the deepest insight into their affair, apart from *Annie Hall*, is an article Allen wrote for the *Kenyon Review* which he included in his third book, *Side Effects*. It's called "Retribution," and centers around the story of an affair the "writer," Harold Cohen, has with a luscious, "blonde, high-cheekboned" actress called Connie Chasen. Harold picks Connie up at a party, and to his surprise she agrees to come home with him immediately, saying, "The truth is, I didn't think I was impressing you." They revel in each other for four weeks. Then those typical autobiographical Allenesque notes start to creep in. "Her shape would have been the envy of a *Vogue* model, and yet an inferiority complex rivaling Franz Kafka's led her to painful bouts of self-criticism. To hear her tell it, she was a dumpy little nonentity, who had no business trying to be an actress, much less attempting Chekhov." The story goes on from there to Harold meeting Connie's WASP family in Connecticut, with her worrying that he will prefer her sister. Actually Harold prefers her beautiful mother, which leads to their breakup, because Connie begins to think of him as a brother and can't have sex with him. Eventually Harold marries Connie's mother, who is into collages and painting.

While there is much in "Retribution" that isn't applicable to the situation between Diane and Woody (certainly Woody never had an affair with Diane's mother), there is much that strikes one as having been taken from his experiences with her: Connie is reading a book of Joseph Heller's and says, "God, you Jews are truly exotic." Harold thinks, "Exotic? She should only know the Greenblats. Or Mr. and Mrs. Milton Sharpstein, my father's friends. Or for that matter, my cousin Tovah. Exotic? I mean they're nice but hardly exotic with their endless bickering over the best way to combat indigestion or how far back to sit from the television set."

Like *Annie Hall*, "Retribution," gives an insight into an affair and the weaknesses, strengths, and insecurities of the protagonists, in a way he couldn't talk about directly, just as Diane probably gives the most unguarded insight into their real-life relationship when talking to *The New York Times* about the popularity of *Annie Hall*: "First it affects couples so much because everybody knows, I think, how difficult it is to have a relationship and to keep it alive and continuing. So there's a universal fact of life that says breaking up happens to everybody, so no one should feel a failure when it does happen.

"Then, it's also sort of Pygmalion, you know. He teaches her and guides her, but then she goes off on her own when she finds the relationship becoming too insular, too confining, too negative, and so she proceeds out into her own life. But in the end they're still friends, they still like each other, and they know they can't go back to the way it once was. That's touching, you know, sort of bittersweet, the idea that you still have a lot of affection for this person but you both know that too much time and change has taken place. But life is time and change, and it just cannot always be worked out, no matter how much affection there may be. I personally feel that I want to have my own life and work and be with somebody who thinks of me as an equal, you know, and that's important for everybody."

4

"OH, YEAH, WOODY'S GIRL?"

Diane wasn't able to prove to the general public that she wasn't *just* Woody's girl until 1977, so that was the way most people thought of her for those seven years. Seven years in which she made good films and bad; gave good performances and bad; seven years that were highlighted by three Woody Allen films, and came to an astounding climax with her fourth film for Allen, *Annie Hall*, and a film for Richard Brooks, *Looking for Mr. Goodbar*.

Her film debut was somewhat inconspicuous. In Cy Howard's film adaptation of the Broadway play, *Lovers and Other Strangers*, a comedy about problems in two families, one Irish Catholic and the other Italian Catholic, Diane played the role of a young bride who becomes disillusioned with her husband and wants to get a divorce. Not an easy thing to do, given the religious and ethnic situation. Although it was a commercial success, the film was not well received by critics. The cast was distinguished, including such veterans as Bea Arthur, Richard

Castellano, Harry Guardino, Anne Jackson, and Gig Young.
Within this august body of comedy actors Diane got lost. She
was hardly, if at all, mentioned in the reviews. Although her
film debut was a great experience, it wasn't the sort of role or
vehicle that would bring her to the attention of the public.
However, it did bring her to the attention of movie producer Al
Ruddy, who decided to test her for a film he was about to make
for Paramount Pictures.

Her second film should have made the public sit up and take
notice, but it didn't. Although it became the most successful
movie in Hollywood history, until the Spielberg blockbusters of
a few years later, Diane was miscast and undistinguished in the
melange of stars and the script of Mario Puzo's best-selling
novel, *The Godfather*. Actually the fault lies less in miscasting
and more in the script, as Carlos Clarens pointed out in *Film
Comment*:

> There are no innocent bystanders in *The Godfather*—no
> bystanders period.
> The one character who could possibly fulfill the function
> gives Coppola the worst trouble: Michael's second wife,
> Kay, who's a New Englander. A film about a society where
> women are subservient need not follow suit in the dramatic
> sense. Kay could have given us an insight, as a surrogate of
> the outside, non-criminal, non-Italian world; instead she is
> made to nag, to act dumb, to have an abortion, which is
> nothing but legalized sin. But worst of all, she is a wraith,
> and Diane Keaton's performance cannot be blamed on any-
> one; there *is* no performance when each shot seems to can-
> cel the preceding.

The part of Kay was important to the balance of the film,
which is most likely why Diane and her manager, Arlyne Rothberg, thought she should do it. But it's easy to understand how
the role got lost in such a sprawling, though brilliant, epic.
Whiz kid director, Francis Ford Coppola (he was only thirty-

two when he made *The Godfather*), has up until recently only made films which are vehicles for men. Although outstanding achievements, if one thinks of the films he has been associated with—*Patton*, which he co-wrote, for an Oscar in screenwriting; George Lucas's *THX 1138*, the first production from his own company, American Zoetrope; the *Godfather* films; and *Apocalypse Now*, to name a few of the first, are all men's films. In his directorial debut for Warner Brothers, the musical *Finian's Rainbow*, was only made to recoup the money on the five-acre "enchanted forest" set built for Joshua Logan's *Camelot*, and Petula Clark wasn't exactly used well.

In *The Rain People*, his personal, penultimate film before *The Godfather*, for which he turned down the job of directing the film version of the musical *Mame* at $400,000, Coppola drew a superb and noteworthy performance from Shirley Knight. But during the course of this film Coppola let her down in the editing by concentrating on James Caan's performance. Perhaps Coppola's overall record in portraying women should have warned Keaton that her starring role in *The Godfather* was not all it was made out to be, but Diane and Arlyne were certainly justified in thinking that she had to do it. Not only was the director being lauded as the most vital young talent in Hollywood, but with the success of the book, Robert Evans and Charles Bluhdorn of Paramount had agreed to a cast that read like a "Who's Who" of Hollywood. Diane would be starring in a movie with Marlon Brando, Robert Duvall, Robert De Niro, and Al Pacino. The only other featured female lead would be Talia Shire (Coppola's sister, who had yet to gain fame in the *Rocky* movies).

In a later interview Diane is quoted as saying, "Right from the beginning I thought I wasn't right for the part," but that was most likely hindsight. After all, it must have been wonderful for the twenty-five-year-old Diane to come back to Los Angeles as a star of a major Hollywood movie. Who wouldn't have accepted the chance, even at the low fee she was getting in this multimillion-dollar production? As Diane said, "Who was I?"

Diane struck up a special relationship with Pacino, and Pacino would enter Diane's life later on, again as her lover, but what may be more important here, is that he reinforced her acting technique by making her more fully aware of Stanislavsky's "Method" than she was under Meisner. A student, convert, and devotee of the teachings of Lee Strasberg, who introduced the Russian Stanislavsky's theories to America (and who, incidentally, made his screen debut in *The Godfather, Part II*), Pacino most probably introduced Diane to Strasberg's Actors Studio. Since then, Diane has taken regular coaching from Marilyn Fried, a member of the studio. While the Actors Studio has possibly been the death of some of its most famous and less famous students, the Method helped Diane tremendously, enabling her to realize her roles and rationalize her insecurities. As she says, "It's very good, because it gives me a handle so that I can be very specific in what I'm doing. And it frees the emotional life."

The Godfather didn't bring Diane the recognition she thought it might. Her role was lost in the overwhelming production, and her recollections of the movie parallel those of the general public. "I don't even remember being in that movie. It was all those guys doing their thing. Remember they even shut the door on me at the end of the first film. That was symbolic of working on the whole movie for me."

Diane has never seen the finished film, and now maintains she always felt she was wrong for the part. Like many actors, she has an aversion to watching herself on the silver screen, but when she feels she is bad in a film she is particularly adverse to seeing it. Since she did have to go back and do some looping (when actors re-dub lines because of technical malfunctions or misguided renderings), Diane *knew* she didn't like herself in *The Godfather*.

"I haven't seen the film. I just decided I would save myself the pain. I had to see a few scenes because I had to loop—dub in some dialogue—and I couldn't stand looking at myself. I thought I looked so terrible, just like a stick in those '40s clothes!" The experience so unnerved her that she never watched herself in any of her early films, not until *Annie Hall*.

These two films notwithstanding, this was the most difficult period of Diane's life. The door shut on her not only in the final scene of the film of *The Godfather*, but also by casting agents, producers, and directors for a period after this most successful film.

Apart from the filming of *The Godfather*, she made only one other film between 1970 and 1973. That other film was Herbert Ross's screen version of *Play It Again, Sam*. She was unemployed for a period of about two-and-a-half-years in all, and this was after she had left Woody and taken on the expense of a two-and-a-half-bedroom apartment in the East Sixties—no small feat, even though rents were lower then. She was also taking acting, singing, and dance lessons every day, so her day-to-day expenses were mounting and she needed work.

It would have been easy for her to have remained "Woody's girl" and relied on his generosity, but that isn't Diane Keaton's way. Instead, relying on her own resources, she found work in the advertising industry, promoting deodorant in television commercials. Originally she didn't want to do them, but the price was right. In the "Hour After Hour" commercials Diane did such horrendous things as play a housewife who runs around a track all day, and then nibbles on her husband's ear when he comes home from work . . . because she is still "fresh as a daisy!" It even got to the point where she jogged around the kitchen in a track suit and then somehow managed to say the line, "Isn't this stuff great!" Housewives in the Midwest loved Diane, so by the end she was getting $25,000 for each commercial. That the concept behind the ads was almost Allenesque in their misguided humor was no compensation, and she passed on the "Hour After Hour" towel to actress Susan Sarandon.

Her fee for the commercials was far more compensation than she received for her first films. For *The Godfather*, for example, she received a paltry $6,000, and for the film of *Play It Again*,

Sam, her remuneration was only $21,500. Yet Diane survived, and she survived without being Woody's girl.

Director Herbert Ross brought together the principals of the Broadway show, including Tony Roberts as Dick and Jerry Lacy as Bogey, in a very faithful film version of Allen's play. Allen plays Allan, a critic for a very highbrow quarterly film review, who (as Allen always is in his roles) is psychologically mixed up. His wife of two years (coincidentally the period of time that Woody and Louise Lasser had been together when he wrote the play) has left him and he has a one-night affair with the equally anxious, Librium-dependent Linda, wife of his best friend, Dick, who's out of town in Cincinnati for the night. Needless to say, Dick comes home early and turns up at Allan's apartment—transposed from Greenwich Village to San Francisco for the film—at which point the plot of *Casablanca* is evoked, with Allen giving an amazing rendition of Humphrey Bogart's last speech from the film.

While drama critic of *The New York Times*, Clive Barnes, had noted her performance in the show, saying, "Diane Keaton is the sweetest little girl as the wayward wife," that newspaper's film critic, Vincent Canby, practically fell in love with her. In his review of May 5, 1972, he said she was excellent and then the next day, in a long article entitled, "Is It Valentine's Day in May?" went on to laud her performance:

> Yet films in both categories occasionally contain performances that, for one reason and another, are interesting enough to deserve attention they will probably never get. . . .
>
> A lovely case in point is Diane Keaton, who plays the suddenly available wife of Woody Allen's best friend in "Play It Again, Sam," now at the Radio City Music Hall. . . .
>
> In "Play It Again, Sam" Miss Keaton (after playing the same role for a year on Broadway) becomes a memorable

comedienne. Watching Miss Keaton . . . one becomes conscious that a real comic intelligence has been waiting for the right material.

Two months earlier, Canby had hardly noticed Diane in *The Godfather*, which made his review and essay on two consecutive days in the *Times* even more telling. The other major critics, likewise, heaped praise on Keaton for *Sam*. Gail Rock, went so far as to say, "Ms. Keaton nearly steals the show. She does it by maintaining a lovely sweet calm in the midst of the madness."

But though the critics loved her, Hollywood wasn't so sure, and Diane was out of work again until the beginning of 1973. In an interview in 1972 with *The New York Times*, she said, "That's a little scary. I say to myself, 'Well, I can last about a year without work.' That's the way I think. I have turned down some things. Some television work. But New York is so expensive!"

It couldn't have been an easy time for her. Critical acclaim doesn't make up for being out of work, but she kept up with learning her craft, continuing to take singing and acting lessons. Every day she would get up and practice singing for an hour because it made her feel good for the whole day—she had accomplished something. But for most of this period of unemployment she would have to keep herself occupied—going to the movies, reading a lot, and doing ordinary household chores. Obviously she would audition, but not getting the roles would make her worried and anxious about her future. She did find strength in analysis, which Woody had introduced her to. The first time she tried it she quit after three sessions because she was scared of the therapist. "I was afraid he didn't like me," she said. Then she found a woman analyst whom she visited three times a week for many years because she felt comfortable with her. "I feel like I can talk to her without her judging me."

Yet Diane's state of mind after finishing *Sam* was so depressed that she again almost considered giving up her profession. "I have this feeling—I don't know if I really want to stay in New

York. My dream has always been to have a house on the ocean in California—not a big one, just a little house with about three or four dogs. And a little old car. That's my dream." Although she adds that something was stopping her and perhaps it was because she needed to get more "straightened out," there was also the lure of a career as well.

Yet she was strong enough to continue to turn down television work. This is understandable. In the hiatus between her first two films she had appeared in such TV series as "Love American Style," "Mannix," and "The FBI," all of which she would rather forget. "'The FBI' one was beyond a shadow of a doubt the worst thing I have ever done. No, I mean it! I was terrible! I was just Blah! No, I think I was worse in 'Night Gallery.' I played a jealous nurse who killed her boyfriend. Or was it the other woman? Anyway, I was unanimously, resoundingly *bad!*"

While keeping her going, these forays into television were not exactly the stuff to draw public attention to Diane, although the TV talk shows she did at the time were. She would say anything that came into her mind, including admitting her affair with Woody as well as their both being in analysis. It gained her a certain notoriety, but she wasn't out for headlines; it was due to her insecurity that she babbled about everything. As she said in an interview to Joan Gage of *The New York Times*, "I feel inadequate on talk shows. I really have nothing to say. And when I get scared, I just giggle and say anything that comes into my head. Once I said—I don't know why—that my grandmother, at seventy-two, had just gotten married and that she and her husband didn't get along. It was true but, of course, my grandmother was crushed."

Much of this was due to naïveté. Television talk show hosts are very clever at what they do—that's how they got to where they are—and Diane felt she had to answer any question that was put to her. She is too astute and experienced to do that now, but her silliness on programs like "The Tonight Show" with Johnny Carson did much to reinforce the public image of her as rather an air-head actress who was simply "Woody's girl." Although the critics were to praise her in her next role—a brain-washed, pseudo-intellectual bimbo from the future—it didn't help the public's perception of her, especially since it was also a Woody Allen film.

Yet it was a noteworthy performance, requiring superb acting technique. This role would mark the beginning of an onscreen actor/director relationship with Woody Allen, through five films during the decade, which would show Diane Keaton to be one of the best screen actresses in the country.

Sleeper opened in December 1973, to a standing ovation at the Coronet Cinema in New York. While very much still in the slapstick tradition of his earlier films, *Sleeper* is a far more mature work than *Bananas* and *Everything You Always Wanted to Know About Sex*. These two films were brilliant in their own way, but relied on one-line gags to carry plots that weren't necessarily as structured as they might have been. *Sleeper* was really the first film in which Allen drew together all the elements of his outstanding talent to make a cohesive whole. He co-wrote the screenplay (his first collaboration with Marshall Brickman), directed, acted in, and even composed the musical score for the film, a tour de force not seen in Hollywood since the early genius of Orson Welles and Charlie Chaplin.

It's worth recalling the plot of the film to show the different levels on which Allen was working. *Sleeper* tells of the misadventures of Miles Munroe, a clarinetist and part owner of the Happy Carrot Health Food Store in Greenwich Village, who is taken to St. Vincent's Hospital for an ulcer operation. He wakes up two hundred years later, in 2173, having inadvertently been cryogenically frozen. Luckily he's been found by scientists who have managed to avoid brainwashing in the perfectly moderated "utopian" America of the future. These "subversive" elements are interested in Miles for his knowledge of the civilization that has been destroyed about one hundred years before, "when a man named Albert Shanker got hold of a nuclear warhead." Naturally individualism (something rather true to Allen's heart) is suppressed in this totalitarian society of the future and the rest of the film recounts his misadventures as he tries to escape the secret police. Along the way he meets up with one of society's leading pseudo-intellectuals, a poetess who is also a hostess. Luna Schlosser (played by Diane) majored in cosmetics, oral sexual technique, and poetry at the university, and really has nothing to say (her poetry reminds one of her friends of Rod McKuen's). Miles takes Luna hostage, falls in love with her, loses her when he's caught and brainwashed, and finds her again when she joins the underground and rescues him. Like most of Allen's films and all great storytelling, the plot outline is simple; it's in the humor that Allen makes an indictment of totalitarian society and shows the possibility of one individual being able to alter the system. While his first three films had wonderful moments and would quote Allen's director heroes, Bergman and Eisenstein, they had less to say than *Sleeper* (although in the eighties *Bananas* seems to be more relevant, with an administration that included a Colonel North and a Central American plot, than it did in the sixties, despite the Bay of Pigs).

Sleeper was Woody's first big budget picture, filmed on location in Colorado and northern California; the production values were such that many people called it Woody's *2001*. The art direction was by Dale Hennesy of *Fantastic Voyage* fame, and the special effects were by A. D. Flowers, who made the *The Poseidon Adventure* so memorable.

The critics either loved or hated *Sleeper*. Pauline Kael, *The New Yorker*'s doyenne of film criticism was particularly hard on it, but those who liked it championed it. Vincent Canby in *The New York Times* compared it to the best of Laurel and Hardy and Jerry Lewis, following up his review with an essay in the Sunday *Times*.

The film is intrinsically hilarious, and some of the comedy scenes reveal the subtle form that Allen's humor would take from then on. For instance, when Miles's brain is being "dewashed," Allen uses psychotherapy as a device, with scenes ranging from Sunday dinner at his parents' house in Brooklyn (a favorite device of his now) to a fragment of Tennessee Williams's *A Streetcar Named Desire*, in which Woody plays Blanche and Diane parodies Brando's Stanley. There is another memorable moment when Woody/Miles imagines himself winning the Miss America Contest.

These were much more intelligent vignettes than Allen's earlier comedic images and required brilliant acting. In *Sleeper*, Diane showed that she could be an outstanding comedienne with considerable range. Canby was to say, "As Woody continues to grow as a filmmaker, so does Diane Keaton continue to develop as an elegant comedienne along the lines of Paula Prentiss and the late Kay Kendall." High praise indeed.

After *Sleeper*, Diane went back to the big Hollywood epic for her next film. One might wonder why Diane decided to do *The Godfather Part II*, especially after the negative critical reception to her first fling as Kay Corleone, but the script of the second *Godfather* film was expected to be far better than the first. In it Coppola intended to examine the motives of all Puzo's characters in a far more profound way. It was also evident from Coppola's latest screenplay, *The Great Gatsby*, that he had become more adroit in achieving a balance between his male and female leads. The women's roles were as sensitively written as the men's, so it was natural for Diane to believe that Kay would be handled more sensitively in *Part II* than in the original *Godfather*.

It's also conceivable that Diane and her manager, Arlyne Rothberg, felt it would look bad if she was the only actor among the principals of the original cast not to do the sequel.

Unfortunately the script didn't live up to her expectations, although Diane was given some fun lines to read—the best being a Bette Davis-like response to Michael Corleone's questioning about Kay's miscarriage. "It was an abortion Michael, just like our marriage is an abortion." *Godfather II* didn't enrich the original; in the words of one critic it "only bracketed it," and for the most part Diane's lines read like cartoon captions—"Oh, Michael, seven years ago you told me you would be legitimate in five years." Obviously, Diane fared as badly in the second *Godfather* as she did in the first, even though the movie was acclaimed, and won most of the Oscars for 1974. Her only recorded comment on the film is a rather succinct "Yeah, and don't forget *Godfather II* where I got slapped. That was good—wow!"

From the fall of 1973, when she finished *Sleeper*, to the late fall of 1974, when she started filming Woody's next project, Diane was mostly out of work. Apart from her scenes in *The Godfather* she returned to her first ambition and was able to book engagements as a nightclub singer. Appearing at such famous clubs as Brothers and Sisters and Reno Sweeney's (a landmark nightclub on West 13th Street in Greenwich Village, which closed at the end of the decade), Diane was also well received as a singer.

It's interesting to note that she was already beginning to build a wall of privacy around herself. Nick Holmes, a singer and songwriter who appeared with her at that time, liked her but found her very introverted. "I don't think she wanted people to know her," he says. "You know, she'd be coy enough to be unbelievable, but it was always attractive enough that you didn't care if it was an act. And I never thought that she herself was aware that she was doing it. Which made it even more attractive. I'd describe her as just being very private."

To illustrate his feelings, Holmes tells that during their breaks between shows, Diane, rather than talking on an intimate level, preferred to play movie games, especially the round-robin game when one person names a film, the next names an actor in that film, another person then names another film that actor has played in, and so on. (These games, which can go on for hours and get very complicated, especially if one gets into the technical people who worked on films, are a favorite of the Hollywood film community.)

Diane was maturing during the early seventies, not only as a person keeping her own confidences, but also as an actress far more aware of her craft. In her next film she would need everything she had ever learned.

Woody Allen's *Love And Death* was a considerable departure from his early work. Slapstick had gone, to be replaced by parody. In this exquisite take-off on Russian literature and theater, his comedy became intellectual. He not only drew from Tolstoy, Chekhov, and Dostoevski, but from his favorite directors, Bergman and Eisenstein, and from the great cinema comedians Groucho Marx and Bob Hope. The film could just as easily have been called "The Road to Moscow," starring the Three Sisters, the Brothers Karamazov, and Buster Keaton, with so many visual and comedic references in a script full of the despair endemic to the Russian soul as perceived in its literature (though, of course, not without a lavish serving of Brooklyn Jewish angst!). The film is simultaneously superbly literate and stupidly funny.

Set in 1812, the film is the story of Boris Grushenko (Woody), a self-avowed coward who is in love with his cousin, Sonja (Diane). Sonja happens to be married to a rich, elderly herring merchant in St. Petersburg, who doesn't exactly appeal to her olfactory senses, and disports herself with every available man in the city. After a brief widowhood she marries Boris, whom she only loves platonically. "Sex without love is an empty experience," she laconically tells Boris. Boris, pausing, rejoins, "But as empty experiences go, it's one of the best." Sonja does, however, enjoy long, meaningful conversations with Boris about the existence of God and the meaning of life, while in fact she's lusting after his brother, Ivan. Whether it's out of patriotic fervor, or simply to get rid of him, she persuades Boris to assassinate Napoleon. Boris, to win her love, agrees, even though he's spent most of the war avoiding the draft rather than fight the French Emperor's Grand Army which is marching on Moscow. Boris gets caught, naturally, and the film ends with him facing the firing squad, though not before he's been double-crossed by a Bergmanesque Angel of Death, who promises him a reprieve at the last moment.

The performances are wonderful, especially Diane's lascivious, intellectual Sonja, and Woody's cowardly but finally brave Boris. It couldn't have been an easy film to make; filming in Paris and Budapest (two locations in which the action never takes place!) in pouring rain, with a crew that couldn't speak a word of English. No one knew what Woody was talking about, let alone understand his humor, so the cast had to play the scenes cold.

"We pretty much lived in a trailer. *Love and Death* was a very isolated film," said Diane just after making it. "Only three people spoke English: Woody, his secretary, and myself. The rest spoke French. Woody speaks French too. We didn't have much to say, so we'd sit in a trailer and talk in between shots, which took forever. And every day we would have the same meal in the hotel. Woody would have fish and I would have chicken, no wine. The waiter thought we were the two most eccentric people in town."

What could have been a marvelous experience for Diane, her first film shoot in Europe, wasn't an easy experience. She should have felt rewarded by the critics' responses.

Vincent Canby in *The New York Times* likened the film to the best work of Buster Keaton, Charles Chaplin, and Jerry Lewis, also writing, "*Love and Death* marks a couple of other advances for Mr. Allen as a filmmaker and for Miss Keaton, as a wickedly funny comedienne." Most of the critics resoundingly agreed with his opinion of the film and Diane's acting, but not all. James Wolcott in the *Village Voice*, while liking the film said, rather pompously, "Her performance in the movie has, as they say, been acclaimed, but on this occasion I decline to rejoice with the common reviewer. I don't think I've ever liked her in a movie: she's brittle, tight-nerved, stannic-voiced. Curved warmth? Not with her—she's all icy angles."

But Wolcott was certainly in the minority, as were Pauline Kael of *The New Yorker*, and John Simon, writing for *New York* magazine, both of whom despised the film. A more typical reaction was that of Mort Sheinman of *Women's Wear Daily*, who wrote, "Ms. Keaton, who has developed a delicious comic talent, has some of the best moments. She can be sexy as well as funny, and, as Sonja, the 'half-saint, half-whore' whose hand and body Boris tries to win, she's irresistible. . . . Together, [Allen and Keaton] may be the best comedy team to come along since the golden days of Sid Caesar and Imogene Coca."

Unfortunately, Diane's next two films made people wonder if it was only with Woody that her talent manifested itself.

Diane set off for Hollywood to do her first film in the film capital. *I Will, I Will . . . For Now*, was also the first film she made in the studio, and the Twentieth Century Fox executives treated her like a star. They believed that Norman Panama's comedy about a couple who divorce and get back together again, despite their sexual problems, would be another *A Touch of Class*, the tremendously successful Glenda Jackson-George Segal comedy, for which Jackson won the Oscar for Best Actress. Unfortunately the script and the chemistry between Keaton and her co-star, Elliott Gould, wasn't right in this rehash of the Rock Hudson-Doris Day comedies of the fifties. When the film came out in February 1976 it was universally panned, Richard Eder in *The New York Times* going so far as to say, "*I Will, I Will* should make people happy that they don't make movies like that anymore."

But before the film came out advance word was so good that shortly after Diane finished shooting in June 1975, Columbia Pictures starred her in another comedy with Gould. Diane had personally enjoyed working with him—because he made her laugh—despite their lackluster onscreen chemistry in *I Will, I Will*. Happily *Harry and Walter Go to New York*, which opened six months after *I Will, I Will*, was far better received—or at least Diane's performance was. It was another big budget film with a superb cast, including James Caan, Michael Caine, Charles Durning, Lesley Ann Warren, and two actresses who would become Diane's greatest friends, Carol Kane and Kathryn Grody.

Harry and Walter, directed rather ineptly by Mark Rydell,

was basically a take-off on *The Sting*, with Caan and Gould as Harry and Walter, two uncouth turn-of-the-century vaudeville actors whose talent lies more in stealing than performing. Unable to make it on Broadway, they decide to turn their attention to obtaining money—by robbing a bank. Not being safecrackers they enlist the services of an elegant international safecracker, Adam Worth (Caine), whom they meet while staying with the editor of an anarchist newspaper, Lissa Chestnut, played by Diane. Ms. Chestnut also needs money to set up a milk fund for New York's poor and inexplicably chooses a small bank in Lowell, Massachusetts, as their target. Keaton, Caine, and Durning (as the lecherous bank manager) were singled out for their performances, but the Caan and Gould roles were hampered by the directing.

While neither of these films, which came out in 1976, were very good, they did quite well at the box office, and kept Diane in the public eye, even if the public still did identify her as Woody's girl. But that would all change in the year in which she made the two most important films of her career.

5

1976

The two-hundredth anniversary of the Republic and the thirtieth anniversary of Diane Keaton was a watershed year for her. She made two of the most important films in her career in 1976, in both giving superlative performances and for one winning the Oscar for Best Actress. Though the actual recognition was nearly a year and a half away, by then she had been recognized by the moviegoing public as one of America's most important film actresses.

Diane actually started out the year by going back to the stage for the first time in six years, in New York at The Circle in the Square. Debbie Wastba, in Israel Horovitz's *The Primary English Class*, was Diane's first role as a teacher that year. Having almost exclusively concentrated on film acting for those intervening years it was a bold move to make. When the reviews came out on February 17, it proved to be a right one. Clive Barnes, the all-powerful theater critic, then still at *The New York Times*, praised her performance in no uncertain terms: "As the beleaguered English teacher, her eyes flashing with despair as things go from bad to worse and from worse to disaster, Diane Keaton gives a delightful portrait of a woman sinking slowly out of control. It is a perfectly judged study in frustration, but she is much aided and abetted by her splendidly zany students."

The play didn't fare quite so well. Horovitz's dialogue, for one thing, was criticized! What's interesting is that Diane was probably already aware that she had lost her feeling for theater. As she said in a recent interview, "I don't like the theater. I really like the movies. I like the fragmented, intimate way of the movies. I like pieces as opposed to a big, long-distance haul. I did a couple of plays and I had a bit of a problem with the audience. I find that the audience is frustrating for me—I have to consider them all. And if you have that attitude you really have to throw your soul onstage, you'll do anything they want. If it was a comedy I was guilty of doing more than I should have done. You know, go over the top a little to get a laugh." She wouldn't attempt acting onstage ever again.

On May 10, the cameras started rolling on a film that Woody had been developing since 1972. He'd originally wanted to shoot it in the summer of 1974, which would have been interesting with regard to Diane's career, as she might have been established as a major star two years before she was.

This was a critical period for actresses in films. Until 1976 there were very few meaningful parts for women in Hollywood, though that year and the next would see such films as *Julia* and *The Turning Point*, which, with *Annie Hall* and *Looking For Mr. Goodbar*, started the trend for "women's films." If Diane had had that 1974 lead on the others, who knows what else she might have done over the next few years—but it's needless to speculate, she was still in two of those pathfinding films!

Diane was certainly aware of the film Woody and Marshall Brickman were working on, because far from being just a lightweight comedienne, who played rather stupid character roles in Allen's films for the past five years, she was also acting as his personal advisor and critic. Right from the beginning he had turned to her for advice. With *Take the Money and Run*, for instance, Allen had no idea how to show a rough cut, and at previews the film would still have the editing chalk marks on it.

Naturally no one laughed; it wasn't until he showed the film to Diane, who said, "This is funny," that he thought he had something that would play. Throughout the seventies she was the only person he would show his screenplays to for comment and advice. (United Artists executives never got to see them, just as Orion executives leave him alone today—probably the only filmmaker whom Hollywood allows this latitude.)

Allen has publicly said, "Diane has been my good luck charm. . . . Since then *[Take the Money]* she's been a consistently clear mind and clear voice on every picture I've made."

There's no doubt that Diane was his muse. And without her, *Annie Hall*, one of the most important films of the decade, would never have been made. It would confirm Allen's status as one of the most important filmmakers in the country, and prove that Diane was an actress and comedienne of substance—as well as turn her into an international celebrity as the progenitor of a new fashion style.

Anhedonia (an inability to experience pleasure) as the film was called up to the last moment (when United Artists executives begged Woody to change the title), was kept secret from the press as long as was possible. This naturally generated even more curiosity and publicity, especially when Woody's film crew was seen all over New York, from Long Island to Coney Island to the Upper West Side. Film crews on location in Manhattan were not as much in evidence as they are now.

The film is, of course, the barely masked account of Diane's love affair with Woody, co-written with his friend Marshall Brickman, as a tribute to Diane. "In *Annie Hall* I was trying to give the audience the view of Diane that I had—the feeling that if they can see her as I see her they will love her." Anyone doubting the intensity of Woody's feelings for Diane, though they had long since ceased to have an actual affair, has only to see the film. As it turned out, audiences did fall in love with her.

Annie Hall is also an affirmation of Woody's respect for Diane and her acting; it is almost, in a way, his present to her of a film that would gain her the highest acting accolades and complete her move to independence, away from being regarded as simply Woody's girl. But the film is far more than that.

The story of Alvy Singer, a neurotic Jewish stand-up comic, and Annie Hall, an actress and nightclub singer, is a story about relationships and how difficult they are to sustain. Reminiscent of Ingmar Bergman's *Scenes From a Marriage*, *Annie Hall* could have been called "Scenes From a Relationship" as it seriously studies, under Woody's wonderful comedy direction, the causes in the breakdown of an affair.

In originally calling the film "Anhedonia," Woody was stating his belief that many relationships are destroyed because one partner or the other can't take pleasure in the other. What makes it more tragic is that Alvy can't take pleasure in the marvelously giddy, but also hopelessly neurotic Annie. He's worried about her not loving him enough, and she's worried about his not being committed enough. (It's beautifully illustrated in one scene, when split-screen they're both talking about their sex life to their shrinks. He says in soulful tone, "Hardly ever, maybe three times a week," and Annie's disgruntled view is, "All the time, at least three times a week.")

There are more differences between them than this, including that of background. He is a Jew from Brooklyn and she is a WASP from Wisconsin (originally the character of Annie was from New York and much harsher, but Woody and Brickman toned her down and made her more appealing). At the end Annie, having had the benefit of Alvy's intellectualism, drifts off—in Alvy's eyes a great backward step—to Los Angeles. He's left to write a play about the affair, which he gives a happy ending, with her coming back to him after an affair with a rock star.

There are some marvelous supporting performances in this insightful portrait of relationships and the society of the seventies: Colleen Dewhurst as Annie's mother; Shelley Duvall as Pam, a one-night stand; Christopher Walken as Annie's brother; Paul Simon; and Diane's friend, Carol Kane, in the role of Allison, Alvy's divorced wife. (It's an indication of Diane's influence on Woody that he cast Kane for this sensitive role, which basically portrays Louise Lasser. Not that Kane isn't a brilliant actress, she is, but having met Diane in *Harry and Walter*, she was then immediately cast in an Allen film.)

Diane, becoming ever more private as a reaction against her growing fame, is loath to admit how closely the story of the neurotic, wonderfully funny, and tenderly sad affair between Alvy Singer and Annie Hall approximated her love affair with Woody. "It's not true, but there are *elements* of truth in it. It's about a relationship and because Woody and I know each other well and have had a relationship, there is a quality of truth in it." She will even go so far as to cite the differences between the script and her real life, but there is still enough truth in the "elements" to suggest that it is what Woody called "loosely auto-biographical," and a relatively close portrait of many aspects of Diane. For example, she does punctuate her speech with "Gees" and "Sures" and "Well, uhs" a lot, though the famous "La de dah" is a script invention; she does sing in nightclubs, as she did at Reno Sweeney and Brothers and Sisters; and she does wear clothes in a totally imaginative and personally chic way that is the ultimate in kooky style. There are also the elements of Woody's now famous portrayal of Grammy Hall, which made Diane's grandmother, Mary, famous, and, Diane and Woody *do* share a terror of live lobsters.

But most important, as in the film, there was a Pygmalion quality to Woody and Diane's affair. Much later, in an interview with critic Gene Siskel of the *Chicago Tribune*, she said, "I see Annie Hall as—gee, this is going to sound awfully cruel—as basically stupid. Maybe unformed and innocent is better. And I think Woody may have seen a little of that in me. It's very much a Pygmalion story, at least in terms of her character." Yet, asked once if Woody was her Professor Higgins, Diane side-stepped the question, like every probe into her private life. "You know I'm not going to say . . . I will only say one thing: Everybody you've been with influenced you in your life in some way."

It's also obvious that by the time Diane made *Annie Hall* everything that Woody had dreamed for her was about to come true. His Eliza Doolittle had grown up completely into a mature beautiful woman. At thirty, Diane, with her auburn hair, perfect complexion, high cheekbones, laughing mouth, and expressive hazel eyes, had grown out of the gawky girl he had first met in *Sam*, and portrayed in *Annie Hall*. She'd been living on her own for about seven years, and was expressing her creativity not just in her singing and acting, but also with her art. One of the bedrooms in her apartment in a magnificent Art Deco building on East 68th Street had been converted into a darkroom, as she was becoming more and more interested in photography. During this time she started two permanent relationships . . . with her cats, Buster Keaton, a red, talkative Abyssinian, and Whitey, an all white, beautiful mixed breed.

White is the color Diane likes to surround herself with. Whether psychologically it's a search for purity, or simply wanting to remove all the extraneous jumble from her life, this apartment (like the Central Park West co-op she would later buy), was white everywhere—walls, ceiling, and floor in every room, looking, as one journalist commented, as if she'd got a bargain deal on white paint somewhere. Even the furnishings were sparse, with two large beige canvas chairs, a matching beige sofa, and several large cacti in the living room. The only relief came from the art, which mainly consisted of examples of her collages and photography, including six dramatic blow-ups of self-portraits she had made in a subway photo machine. It would seem to be the apartment of someone searching for the truth about herself, and certainly Diane was as interested in experiencing and expressing herself in her art as she was in her acting. In fact, during the shooting of *Annie Hall* she went so far as to enroll in a print-making course at the New School on West 12th Street in Manhattan. But when she got there her nerve failed her and she couldn't even walk into the classroom, which is quite amazing for someone who so generously shows as much of herself as she does in her films, especially as she did in *Annie Hall*.

For Diane one of the best things about the film was that she played a nightclub singer, singing stylized versions of "Seems Like Old Times" and "It Had To Be You" in her light, melodic voice. The exposure of her private life was something else she found inhibiting. As she confided to Rex Reed, "It is always embarrassing to reveal my personal life . . . but emotional embarrassment is a condition of acting . . . revealing yourself even when you're not playing your own life. . . . The biggest worry I had making *Annie Hall* was whether or not I would get in my own way. I was afraid that unconsciously I might stop myself from showing the truth because it made me uncomfortable. But the whole process of acting is uncomfortable anyway."

Annie Hall had a much longer shooting schedule than Allen normally requires, and he ended up with over 100,000 feet—roughly fifty hours—of film which he and editor Ralph Rosenblum, would have to cut down to 94 minutes. (Woody quipping, "I love to annihilate film when we're cutting it!") It took them four months to edit it and the film wasn't ready until a month before the premiere at the Los Angeles Film Exposition on March 27, 1977.

In the meantime Diane had gone on to start filming the most difficult role of her career, one in which she would have to expose herself even more than she had done before, both literally and figuratively. This was the dramatic role of Theresa Dunn in Richard Brooks's film version of Judith Rossner's best-selling novel, *Looking For Mr. Goodbar*.

Diane had gotten what was the most sought-after role in moviedom that year. Maverick sixty-seven-year-old director Richard Brooks was one of the most respected people in the industry (the writer and/or director of such films as *Key Largo*, *Blackboard Jungle*, *Cat on a Hot Tin Roof*, *Elmer Gantry*, and *In Cold Blood*), and the story of a demure, repressed Catholic school teacher of the deaf with a disability due to childhood poliomyelitis, who predatorily stalks single bars by night for sexual thrills, was a part that every major actress in Hollywood wanted to get her teeth into. Brooks interviewed many actresses, and daily there were items in the gossip columns that stated that everyone from Sally Field to Barbra Streisand had been signed. Ever a rebel, Brooks didn't want a big name—and the budget was small at $2.3 million, with himself getting only a "scale" fee of $12,000 (plus a percentage of the profits), and his leading lady would be paid only $50,000, though that didn't seem to deter the big names, who knew a great role when they saw it.

It was Freddie Fields, the producer of *Goodbar*, who suggested to Brooks that he interview Diane, and based on some footage he saw of her in *Harry and Walter* he agreed to talk to her, but frankly he wasn't sure she had the range. As Brooks told *The Boston Phoenix*, at first he felt Diane was shy and inarticulate (as most people assume first meeting Diane cold), but then he began to see she had something else, an inner steel and great determination, and he could see that she wanted to get away from being cast as a light comedienne. "I thought she could play the part," recalls Brooks. "I knew she could play the teacher part. The other side I didn't know, but who knows that sort of thing until you start to do it." It was a role Diane desperately wanted, but Brooks, carefully, refused to allow her to read for the role. "No, it's too early," said Brooks. "Let's wait a while and talk again. I don't know who you are! I don't know what makes you tick, what you're afraid of—nothing!" They met again a few weeks later in a restaurant in Los Angeles and talked about everything under the sun . . . except the film. And Brooks, while sure she could play Theresa, still wasn't sure she could play "Terry," in the bar and bedroom scenes.

He also wasn't sure that she was beautiful enough for the role; she was too nice. So he continued his search, interviewing other actresses. But something kept bringing him back to Diane, and he decided to interview her again. Then it struck him that she was exactly the type of person the story was about, someone nice looking and sexy, "but not the best-looking person in the class. Someone you would almost overlook."

Brooks decided to give Diane a chance to read the script—

something he normally didn't do. Usually his actors get to see the script just before filming a scene, and then it's taken away from them to be shredded because of his preference for secrecy and noninterference from the studio. He made Diane read every part in the film to see if she understood the characters. He told the *Phoenix:* "It was tough for her; she was embarrassed by some of it, it upset her. But it was good too; she began to care about Terry, she began to like that girl."

In one of their interviews the veteran filmmaker turned to her and without preamble said, "Look, there's going to be some tricky lighting in this movie, and I've got to start thinking about how to photograph your body. And, well, Diane, I'm going to have to see what you look like." After a shocked silence, Diane quietly said, "O.K., Brooks."

Diane was offered the coveted role, but then she began to get doubts herself. She was worried about the nude scenes and worried about having to make love to an actor she didn't like personally, and Brooks allowed her a say in who would play opposite her. The rest of the characters had been cast. Richard Kiley would play Theresa's Irish-American cop father, now ill; Tuesday Weld, the fun-loving and uninhibited elder sister, Katherine, who has to go to Puerto Rico for an abortion; Alan Feinstein, the college professor who is her first love; William Atherton, the boring but correct Catholic lawyer she's supposed to marry, and Tom Berenger, the pickup who finally kills her. All that remained was to cast Tony, the Vietnam vet, Italian-American stud who takes Terry to heights of sexual ecstasy, with some rather forceful foreplay. Brooks finally cast Richard Gere, whom he'd never met, but had liked in Terrence Malick's *Days of Heaven.*

Diane was still unsure of her ability to play the role, so finally Brooks asked her straight out, "Do you really want to do this?" Diane said she did, but could she talk it over with some people. As Brooks recalled for the *Phoenix,* he replied, "You talk this over with your analyst, and I'll throw you off the movie." Diane spoke to Woody, who was all for it, and then she spoke to her father, asking him what he would say if he saw her nude on the big screen. Jack replied, "Is it necessary? Do you trust this guy who's directing? If you do, then take the part."

Diane prepared herself carefully for the film, though not by on-site research. The shy woman who was afraid to go into a classroom that summer wasn't exactly about to traipse into New York's singles bars, telling one interviewer evenly, "I've never picked up a man in my life." Instead she worked with the sensory exercises her coach Marilyn Fried suggested, which the Actors Studio uses to relax people. "In *Mr. Goodbar* I used them to try to touch those parts of myself that dealt with sexuality. I wanted to get as far as I could into feelings of pain, and what that meant to Theresa Dunn, and how I as a person could come on to somebody. I worked on it by myself, and eventually got to feel, to imagine, how it is to pick up a man. But it would be a lie to say I totally became the part, to say, 'Yes, I am the part.'"

She also quite candidly admitted that she had had fantasies about picking up men. "Almost every woman I've talked to identifies with her enormously." She told *The New York Times*, "In their fantasies, everybody's been hurt, everybody's been mad at men, everybody feels a kind of longing to belong. Picking up a man in a bar is definitely an idea I've had in my mind, so the movie was a great opportunity to play out all those things."

But Diane was again to have trepidation just before they started filming in Chicago. Brooks turned to her and said roughly, "Now's the time to pull out, Diane. I can still get someone else. You've got to be absolutely *sure*. Rehearsing these scenes is going to be embarrassing. You're going to have to do it over and over again. There are going to be technicians there. A guy is going to have to run a tape measure from the camera to your buttocks to get the focus right. They're going to treat you like a piece of meat. Diane, can you take it?" Diane burst into tears, but she had to guts to say, "Let's go, let's do it."

She could and she did. In an exhausting schedule of seventy-six days she was on the set every single day, even after her rib was broken in a fight scene with Gere. Obviously some scenes were more difficult than others, such as a fight involving a switchblade, which was difficult for Diane, who loathes violence. When she couldn't go through with her first sex scene with the college professor, Brooks sent her back to her dressing room and put a jazz rendition of Bach on the tape recorder. After a while, Diane came out of her dressing room and asked about the music, which she found beautiful, saying, "If you let that music play on the set, I think I can do it." She did it.

She also found it upsetting when Brooks took her to a hospital to show her a child in a full body cast; the character Theresa had suffered polio as a child. Diane couldn't stand the sight of it and started to cry, but Brooks ordered her to stay and look at the girl, telling her that that was why Theresa wanted to live so much and enjoy life. He also told her to stop crying because Terry didn't cry; she had to be stronger than that. Diane never cried again on the set.

Brooks's methods of getting the performance out of Diane weren't all shock tactics. One time he wanted her to come out of the bathroom set with a look of sexual anticipation on her face, at the thought of the naked man waiting on the bed, but the bed was off camera (and empty) and Diane couldn't come up with the emotion. So he told her to go back into the bathroom, and while she was there he took off his shirt. Then, when she came back through the door he was busily removing his pants. Diane simply broke out laughing, and when she came out again she was perfectly composed and had exactly the look Brooks wanted from her!

At the end of the exhausting filming, her tough, irascible director had nothing but praise for her, telling *Newsweek*, "You can sleep next to a person for forty years and not know what they're like inside. Diane invites you into her and exposes all of herself." For the *Time* cover story on Diane in September 1977, he said, "She has more artistic courage than anyone I know."

OSCAR

He stands thirteen and a half inches high and his tin, copper, and gold-plated body weighs six and three-quarter pounds. After the Nobel Prize, this statuette of a naked man plunging a sword into a reel of film is probably the most famous award in the world. Despite his nickname, supposedly given to him by Bette Davis because his buttocks reminded her of those of her second husband, Herman O. (Oscar) Nelson, he's the most prestigious award in entertainment, instantly bequeathing on his recipients respect, recognition, and star status of the highest order, not to mention financial bankability.

When Diane's two 1976 films came out in April and October of 1977 to universal critical acclaim for her performances, there wasn't a doubt in the mind of Hollywood, the critics, and moviegoers that she would be nominated as Best Actress. But for which film, or perhaps, unprecedentedly, for both?

Annie Hall's reviews were quite extraordinary; rarely has any film comedy been given such in-depth analysis in the media, who regarded it as a step forward in American filmmaking. There were the obvious comparisons to Ingmar Bergman, with Woody being saluted as the American equivalent of the Swedish master. Vincent Canby, in *The New York Times*, wrote a critical essay explaining why this was so. *Variety* started its review with the paragraph:

In a decade largely devoted to male buddy-buddy films, brutal rape fantasies, and impersonal special effects extravaganzas, Woody Allen has almost single-handedly kept alive the idea of heterosexual romance in American films.

This important trade paper went on to say, "His four romantic comedies with Diane Keaton strike a chord of believability that makes them nearly the only contemporary equivalent of the Tracy-Hepburn films." The *Wall Street Journal* not only called the film "the best movie romance in a long time," but defined Woody's comedy as art, and said that Diane played "with exquisite comic flair." Andrew Sarris, the noted film critic of the *Village Voice*, gave away the secret that the film, before it was cut to ninety-four minutes was intended to be a far more serious work, but then forgave Allen for "the cinematic valentine he has woven for Diane Keaton." The *Los Angeles Times* ended its review with "The standing ovation you hear is not only for the feat, but for the art of it."

And so the press went on. But perhaps more important was the reaction of the general public: lines formed around the block at every theater it played in, people would return to see the film three or four times; and they would stand and cheer at many of the special moments, especially for Diane.

Diane became a media sensation; just as Woody predicted, everyone who saw her fell in love with her. The "Annie Hall look" of crumpled men's chinos, an oversized man's white shirt, a vest, and a loud, large tie loosely knotted became *the* fashion expression of the season. Fashion designers copied her, and Diane did as much for pants for women as Marlene Dietrich and Katharine Hepburn had before her.

Diane, of course, modestly understated her effect on the fashion world. "Yeah, sure, for a little while, not very long. It wasn't like the Hula Hoop. It was a nice little thing. I came up the gradual way. I never was like John Travolta—I wasn't a big sexual star that was idealized." But she was wrong. Young women everywhere were going about not only dressed like her but quoting her—"La de dah!" To this day her acute style sense has been closely watched by the fashion world for whatever trend she will set next.

By the end of the summer every magazine in the country wanted to get ahold of her for a cover story or a fashion layout, but Diane was too shy and insecure—and too clever—to allow this to happen. She gave only four major interviews, to *The New York Times*, the New York *Daily News*, with Rex Reed, *Rolling Stone*, and finally, in September, *Time* magazine, for one of their coveted cover stories. With *Time*'s colossal circulation and worldwide distribution, this would make her a recognized name around the world. It was enough and it whet the public's curiosity for more. But Diane was not giving any more, especially about her private life, and she wasn't about to become a clothes horse. She'd done that for *Vogue* back in the dark days of the beginning of the decade when she was out of work.

For one thing, Diane couldn't see herself becoming the next Farrah Fawcett-Majors, whose golden tresses, strong jaw, and sumptuous body were staring out from every magazine cover on every newsstand in the country that year. As Diane's manager, Arlyne Rothberg put it, perhaps *slightly* unfairly, "The only people who need publicity are people without talent." Diane's viewpoint was that she didn't have, well, the *attributes* Farrah had, and she couldn't see why anyone would want her for countless covers anyway, not that she was going to do them. Because, according to Arlyne, "The *Time* interview was the most painful experience she's had so far." That sounds like agent-ese though; *Goodbar* surely caused her more mental anguish than questions from the *Time* reporters.

Meanwhile Diane went about her daily tasks, taking lessons from Marilyn Fried, singing lessons from Janet Frank, exercise classes at the New York Health Club, as well as visiting her analyst, taking photographs, and taking some "quality time" with Buster and Whitey.

After *Annie Hall* premiered, Rothberg's office was inundated with scripts. At least twenty a week would pile up for Diane, and in August it was rumored that she was being considered for the lead in the film of Joshua Davis's novel *Life Signs*. It was a strong role, but the deal fell through when her agents, of the William Morris Agency, asked for $750,000 for Diane's fee and Rothberg, who, though she vehemently denies it, insisted on co-producing the film. Whatever the reasons, Diane didn't make *Life Signs*, and decided to do Woody's next film instead. It wasn't a comedy this time and would, according to Woody, be a "far more heavy and tortured and difficult" role than *Goodbar!*

In the last week of September the *Time* story came out. It was obvious that the newsweekly's reporters loved Diane, using such adjectival phrases as, ". . . a dizzying grin that spreads and resonates like the sound of trumpets blown at dawn by celestial heralds." Certainly more florid than *Time*'s usual succinct style! Perhaps Diane didn't quite realize what this would do for her; when she accompanied Woody to the opening night of the New York Film Festival that same week, dressed as she normally did, à la Annie Hall, the five hundred-or-so guests dressed to the nines just stopped and stared. One could have heard a pin drop; it was like two different species looking at each other through the bars in a zoo. Diane did a long slow take and said, "Oh, wow," before she and Woody sidled to the nearest corner to hide. They left shortly thereafter; Diane simply couldn't handle being the center of all that attention.

Just about the time Diane was to start the new Woody Allen project at the end of October, *Looking For Mr. Goodbar* opened. It caused even more of a furor in the entertainment pages of every newspaper and magazine than *Annie Hall* had. Not because it was liked, but because it was so universally hated! Vitriol poured out in printing ink against Brooks's portrayal of heterosexual and homosexual pickup bars and "squalid sex." The film was possibly the most outspoken realization of this seamy fact of nightlife ever, and the critics took a stance that was holier than thou, though at least the more responsible of them realized it was a film noir. Those with reviews that were more tempered included *Variety*, *The New York Times*, the *Daily News*, the *Christian Science Monitor*, and the English film magazine, *Sight and Sound*. Even Frank Rich in *Time* magazine hated the film, though he, like nearly every one else, praised Keaton.

While the critics may have loathed the film, everyone recognized Diane's performance as a tour de force. Those who hadn't recognized her talent before "suddenly" discovered her, and her long-standing champions like Vincent Canby were in a position of being able to say, "I told you so." Diane was acclaimed as a rare talent who could play anything, from light comedy to intense drama. Adjectives like "Extraordinary," "Sensational," "Electrifying," and "Provocative" were used to describe her performance—much to the benefit of Paramount's advertising campaign. One critic even put his soul in hock, so dazzled was he by her acting; Rex Reed wrote, "If Diane Keaton doesn't win an Oscar for *Looking for Mr. Goodbar*, there is no God."

The public, either fascinated or repelled by what they'd heard about the film went, like lemmings, to see it in droves. That fall, Diane was the queen of the big screen, despite wonderful performances by Jane Fonda, Vanessa Redgrave, Anne Bancroft, and Shirley MacLaine. In everyone's minds she was the all-out favorite for the Academy Award for her performance in *Goodbar*.

Meanwhile Diane held herself aloof from all the speculation, quietly acting the difficult role of Renata in Woody's first serious—that is, without comedy—film.

As Vincent Canby so cleverly described the culture shock that *Interiors* was to Allen fans, "Not to be prepared for it is to embark on a Miami beach vacation having just taken a total immersion course in 17th-century English literature." *Interiors* is more Bergman than Bergman, and was Woody's best film to date. Stunningly photographed by Gordon Willis, Allen, as director, showed the spatial relationships between his principals visually as well as he did their inner thoughts in the script, which was a solo effort. *Interiors*, set primarily in a spacious, open, Long Island beach house and a New York apartment, decorated within an inch of its life, is about a family trapped within their wealthy environment and their relationships with one another, all of them longing to get out.

The patriarch of the family, Arthur (E.G. Marshall), a successful lawyer, is fed up with his neurotic interior decorator wife, Eve (Geraldine Page). She is determined to keep her husband and her three daughters, Renata, a kind-of-successful poet who writes for *The New Yorker*; Joey (Marybeth Hurt), an aspiring-artist-with-no-talent youngest daughter, who is her father's favorite; and Flyn (Kristin Griffith), a beautiful-but-shallow actress who's a success in bad television movies and who snorts cocaine. Then there is Arthur's mistress, Pearl (Maureen Stapleton), a big, breezy woman, as vulgar as her name, who at least lives life to the fullest, and has got more sense, even if it's horse sense, than all of them put together, except perhaps Arthur, who at least has the gumption to get out, divorce Eve, and marry Pearl.

Renata is unhappily married to Frederick (Richard Jordan), an unsuccessful novelist who drinks, and Joey is having an unsuccessful relationship with a filmmaker, Mike (Sam Waterston), whom she finally marries. (And so it goes on.) The irony in Woody's portrayals of our trapped society does indeed make the film bleak, but *Interiors* is an all-too-real study of people who only know how to exist, and not how to live.

The role of Renata was challenging and daring for Diane to play in that she had to express inner creativity while looking rather woebegone. It was her most cerebral and understated performance to date. Woody had penned the role especially for Diane. In analysis and plagued by fantasies of death and metaphysical despair, one can see what Woody means by saying, "Renata speaks for me, without question. She articulates all my concerns." Renata was a valentine of another kind to Diane. Here, Woody was showing to the world what a great serious actress she is.

*   *   *

When the Academy Award nominations were announced in February 1978 there were few surprises. It looked as though *Star Wars*, the most popular film of the year (overtaking *The Godfather* and *Gone With the Wind* as the all-time highest grossing film), would sweep the awards. The second most popular film of the year was acknowledged with a Best Actor nomination for John Travolta in *Saturday Night Fever*. And, of course, *Annie Hall* was nominated in several categories. What surprised nearly everyone was that Diane was nominated for *Annie Hall* and not *Goodbar*. (Whether Mr. Reed can use this as proof of the nonexistence of a Supreme Diety is difficult to ascertain!) The competition for Best Actress was fierce; in the first year of strong women's roles for a long time, Diane was pitched against Anne Bancroft and Shirley MacLaine for *The Turning Point*, Marsha Mason for her husband Neil Simon's *The Goodbye Girl*, and Jane Fonda for *Julia*. (Inexplicably, Vanessa Redgrave was nominated in the Best Supporting Actress category for *Julia*, even though her name was "above the title.")

At about five o'clock on March 29, 1978, in late afternoon sunshine in downtown Los Angeles, the limousines began to pull up at the Dorothy Chandler Pavilion for the Awards ceremony. The crowds were roaring, partly because Herbert Ross was using the event as a location for filming Michael Caine and Maggie Smith in a sequence for Neil Simon's *California Suite*, and partly because BIMBO (Blacks in Media Broadcasting Organization) and the Jewish Defense League were protesting Vanessa Redgrave, while the PLO was across the street applauding her! Broadcast live by ABC Television and beamed across the world to billions of viewers at home, things got off to a bad start almost immediately. Host Bob Hope came out and referred to the previous Academy Award winners who had just been onstage, including Bette Davis and Gregory Peck, as "the road company of the Hollywood Wax Museum," which wasn't exactly kind given his own seventy-four years. His opening monologue was equally offensive, with one-line gags such as "Liz Taylor's back on her farm in Virginia . . . still trying to milk a chicken." Mind you, Richard Burton, in the audience and one of the nominees for Best Actor in *Equus*, seemed to find it hilarious, and Woody, the most nominated person that year, might have enjoyed the one-liner from his hero, Hope, if he had been there.

The new heartthrob, John Travolta, presented the Best Supporting Actress Award. When the envelope was opened the winner was Miss Redgrave, for *Julia*. And then commenced one of the most famous or infamous moments of Academy Award show lore. Redgrave's acceptance speech seemed like a PLO political manifesto, which in the predominantly Jewish-controlled film industry was not a wise thing to do. (Actually, if one examines the text of the speech, it never mentions the PLO at all, and is really an indictment of anti-Semitism and fascism, as was Lillian Hellman's story, *Julia*. But it didn't come across that way to an audience that was waiting for the outspoken English actress to make a radical statement.)

Luckily, the next presenters were R2D2 and C-3PO, with Mark Hamill in attendance, to give the Special Achievement Award, which lightened up things a bit, especially when they met up with the fifty-year-old Mickey Mouse, who was making his entrance as they were going offstage. From then on events proceeded relatively calmly, although Hope made a crack about Jason Robards not being there to receive the Best Supporting Actor Award, suggesting he was playing bridge with Marlon Brando and George C. Scott (two famous nonattendees), while in fact he was on the Broadway stage in an O'Neill play.

At long last came the Awards everyone in the auditorium and the billions of people watching on their home screen had been waiting for: Best Director, Best Screenplay, Best Actress and Actor, and Best Film. When veteran director King Vidor and actress Cicely Tyson announced the award for Best Director . . . Woody Allen for *Annie Hall*, there was a hush, not just because everyone thought George Lucas would win for *Star Wars*, but because no one came up to accept the Oscar. For Best Original Screenplay . . . at least Marshall Brickman was there to accept it on his and Woody's behalf.

Then Walter Matthau and Janet Gaynor, the first Best Actress Winner, came out to announce the winner of what was still a close race for Best Actress of the year, despite Diane having already been awarded the prestigious Golden Globe, New York Film Critics, and National Film Critics awards for her portrayal of Annie Hall.

The applause for Diane was thunderous, yet Diane seemed shocked and stunned. As a result of her disbelief, she fell back into her pattern of inarticulation; her acceptance speech was short, with all the embarrassing mannerisms one associates with her. Giggling with embarrassment, she said, "It's simply terrific . . . This is something . . ." Then she praised her fellow nominees, and concluded, "I would just like to say thanks to Woody and thank you, thank you very much."

Diane's peers, the Academy members, had deemed her worthy of the highest recognition they could give her.

Richard Dreyfuss won for Best Actor in *The Goodbye Girl*, with more votes than Burton, Travolta, and Allen, and then it was time for Best Picture. Nominated were *Annie Hall*, *The Goodbye Girl*, *Julia*, *The Turning Point*, and *Star Wars*. It seemed to be a foregone conclusion that *Star Wars* would win, but when the envelope was opened by Jack Nicholson it was *Annie Hall*, the first comedy to win Best Picture since *Tom Jones* in 1963, fourteen years before. Luckily the Best Picture category is accepted by the producers, and Jack Rollins and Charles H. Joffe had that pleasure.

In all the furor over Vanessa Redgrave's speech, no one noticed the impolite snub that Woody had made to the Academy. He was too busy that night, playing jazz in New York at Michael's Pub as he always does on Monday evenings, to know that he had won and that *Annie Hall* had walked off with all the major Oscars, beating the sure favorite, *Star Wars*, until he read it in the papers the next morning. While he later said he was happy for Brickman, Joffe, and Diane, at the time he made no statement to the press. It must have been very disheartening for Diane, although she did get to take her favorite, youngest sister, Dorrie, to the ceremony. While it's well known that Woody doesn't like the Awards, one would think that he could have made an effort for once, especially for Diane.

7

WARREN

The complete opposite of the frail, short Woody Allen, Warren Beatty, with a six-foot-two, one hundred and eighty pound, *very well-distributed* frame, is every woman's dream of the ideal matinee idol. Tall, dark, smoldering, and handsome, his reputation with the opposite sex is long, varied, and *very* talked about.

Diane Keaton seemed like the most unlikely match for Warren, not possessing the apparent beauty of, say, Natalie Wood, Joan Collins, Leslie Caron, or Julie Christie, to name but four of the longer-lasting in a long string of his girlfriends. A constant womanizer and always in the limelight, one would have thought that the outwardly shy, retiring Diane would be the last person to appeal to Warren Beatty.

But although they form the basis of sexual attraction, outward appearances and reputations are deceptive. There's no doubt that Diane and Warren were attracted to each other from the first time they met. What was it that they saw in each other?

At first glance, Warren is so obviously different from Woody, although Diane told Joan Gage of *The New York Times* in 1972:

"I've always thought [Woody] was kind of cute. Gorgeous men always put me off. I think in all my life I've only had one gorgeous boyfriend. One. But when you get to know someone very well, his face changes." This could have been Diane defending her relationship with Woody; after all, she admits that in high school she was always mooning over the handsome jocks on the basketball team—and Warren is undoubtedly athletic. One has to accept that the physical side of Warren appealed to the Diane who never got the boys she secretly desired as a teenager. His attention must have been tremendously flattering.

However, there is another side to Warren that the public hardly ever sees. He is a shy, retiring person of considerable intellect with knowledge on a vast range of subjects. Though far more mature and worldly than when she met Woody, Diane was engaged in a constant search to better herself and make up for her lack of formal education and Warren must have appealed to her thirst for knowledge.

It is also interesting that Warren was the same age as Woody, eleven years older than Diane. She may still have been looking for the right man to take care of her. Warren was also a filmmaker of formidable reputation.

For his part, as Leslie Caron has astutely observed, Warren has a penchant for Academy Award–winning actresses—she should know, being the first of two of his great loves, the other being Julie Christie, who attracted him after they won Oscars. Warren, perhaps because he had never won Academy recognition for his work, was impressed by people who had, and needed to prove to himself that he was as good as they were. With women, the best way he could do that was by making them fall in love with him. This is the side of Warren that is basically insecure and needs to be rewarded.

Warren is also attracted to strong women. It's not without reason that Leslie Caron, when she was married to Peter Hall, then director of the Royal Shakespeare Company in England, was known as "The French Witch," a veiled reference to Margaret of Anjou, Edward IV's wife, who did much to cause the War of the

Roses. And, as we have seen, under that scatterbrained persona the public perceived Diane to be, there was a strong, independent, outspoken woman. And, last but not least, Diane's beauty, while not classical, is extraordinary. Just to see her eyes and feel the warmth of her smile is enough to turn any man's head.

Diane and Warren's relationship was so strong that at one point many Hollywood insiders were positive that she had finally tamed the beast and that they would be married. It wasn't to be. Diane has been quoted in the *National Star* as saying, "Liking a person and loving a person don't seem to go together. When you love, you get possessive and jealous, and when those feeling . are gone, you don't want to see each other anymore. If I wasn't an actress, I'd probably be married, unhappily. I think I need a nicer opinion of myself before I marry. When it comes to me, I like to take my time."

Yet, for a couple of years, Keaton and Beatty were inseparable, a constant source of titillation for the gutter press. Although Diane continued to live in New York, she spent a lot of time at Beatty's mansion on the crest of the Hollywood hills on Mulholland Drive above Beverly Hills. And the depth of her feelings for Beatty is evident in that she started to look for a large co-op to replace her small apartment on East 68th Street. Quite a few New York realtors were surprised when they realized that the quiet, bespectacled man with her was Warren Beatty. With Diane, he became much more secure and for much of the time they were together stopped chasing starlets.

The romance began when Diane won the Oscar. Richard Brooks, who had directed Warren in *$ (Dollars)*, a spy spoof made in England with Goldie Hawn, had drawn Warren's attention to Diane for her performance in *Goodbar*. Long before the next Oscar ceremony in March 1979, the month in which Warren and Diane visited Russia to scout locations for *Reds*, they obviously had become an item. On that Awards evening, Warren's sister, Shirley MacLaine, who supposedly doesn't like her brother very much, took great delight in maliciously joking about his "Don Juan" reputation, much to Diane's great embarrassment as the cameras zoomed in on her blushing face for the millions of viewers at home.

Warren hadn't always been the great stud. Believe it or not, young Henry Warren Beaty (he changed the spelling later) was a shy little boy, constantly overshadowed by his tomboyish older sister, Shirley, and his strict, intellectual, and accomplished parents. Born on March 31, 1937, he grew up as an introverted child, at home and at school. His mother, Kathlyn MacLaine, was a school teacher from strong Scots-Canadian stock who had taught acting in Nova Scotia, Maryland, and West Virginia. She met Ira Owens Beaty when she went to Maryland College to teach drama; he was a professor of psychology and education there. A retiring but authoritarian large man, whose passion was the fiddle, Ira had settled for studying philosophy at Johns Hopkins rather than succumb to the lure of performing as a solo violinist in Europe. The young couple moved to Richmond, Virginia, and settled into the traditional lifestyle of the capital of the old Confederacy where Ira eventually became superintendent of Richmond High School.

Their children were the antithesis of each other. Shirley was outgoing and athletic, batting up a storm on the softball field, and also more theatrically inclined, having shown early promise in singing and dancing. Her parents, frustrated performers themselves, encouraged this in both children, seeing in them the realization of their frustrated dreams. Indeed, such was their ambition that Shirley remembers being berated so severely by her father because he had found her high school performance as Ado Annie in *Oklahoma* lacking that she vomited from crying so much.

Henry was quieter. Although he excelled at the piano, he was introverted and shy, preferring to go to his "private place," a closet off his bedroom that had a window, and dream. But inside, "the Kid," as he was nicknamed and is still known by close friends, wanted to perform as much as Shirley. He would mime to Al Jolson records in the basement and memorized the complete works of Eugene O'Neill.

During puberty, little Henry came out of his chrysalis and developed into a strapping young man. On the challenge of one of his masters, he gave up books for sports and discovered he was a natural athlete. By the time he graduated from Washington and Lee High School in Arlington, Virginia, he had been offered ten football scholarships by various colleges. As an incredibly handsome young jock, he also discovered that he was the human male equivalent of catnip to girls.

Shirley had already left home to go to New York to be a dancer. It is said that her father disapproved, although this could have been more a case of jealousy than disappointment. Both his children seemed bent on taking up the theatrical profession which he had chosen to suppress. In 1955, Henry Warren chose to study acting at Northwestern University in Evanston, Illinois, rather than take a football scholarship and study law as his father wanted. The year before, Henry had been bitten by the acting bug when he took a summer job with the National Theater in Washington, D.C., as a rat catcher. The theater had been infested by rats and one of the actors had been bitten. Two hundred and five pound Henry, who wanted any job in the theater, was hired to stay outside in the alley and kill rats while inside Helen Hayes gave a triumphant performance in Thornton Wilder's *The Skin of Our Teeth*.

At that time Northwestern had a reputation as one of the best colleges in the country in which to study acting. Alvina Krause, the drama professor, had been responsible for starting the careers of such actors as Charlton Heston, Patricia Neal, and Ann-Margret. But the School of Speech at the college didn't meet Warren's standards, and he dropped out after a year, just as Diane had dropped out of her colleges.

Shirley, in a coincidental parallel to Diane's career, got the lead in her first musical, *The Pajama Game*, when Carol Haney injured her leg. Warren decided to follow his sister to New York; after all if she could do it, so could he. Surprisingly, his parents, like Diane's, supported his decision, and agreed to finance him to a certain extent. Adding the second *t* to his name, he came to New York as Warren Beatty, and started to look for work as an actor. Considering his almost complete lack of experience, it seems like total madness in retrospect, but Warren, with his supreme outward confidence, felt he was ready. He took lessons at the Stella Adler studio, but jobs in the theater were just as hard to get then as now; despite his looks, Warren had to resort to manual labor, working on the third bore of the Lincoln Tunnel, washing dishes, and playing the piano in cocktail bars. Slowly, between 1957 and 1959 it began to pay off and he started to get small roles in television.

His big break came when he appeared in a stock company production of *Compulsion* in New Jersey, and was spotted by the brilliant director Joshua Logan, who wanted an unknown for a movie he was to direct, *Parrish*. Warren was flown to Los Angeles to test with another novice, Jane Fonda. He didn't get the role, but MGM offered him a five-year contract at $400 a week. Warren was then twenty-two, and with no real experience this seemed to be the start of his career. So what did he do but read the first script they offered him and turn it down! Thus began a pattern he would follow all his life.

He borrowed money to break his contract and came back to New York. While in Hollywood, he had read for William Inge's *Splendor in the Grass*, which Elia Kazan was to make. In Manhattan, he found the film had been postponed, but Inge had been so impressed with him that he cast Warren in the leading role in his new play, *A Loss of Roses*. Here his already "difficult" reputation went from bad to worse as he argued with everyone from the director downwards; his co-star, Shirley Booth, quit the show before it opened because of his antics. *A Loss of Roses* (ironically now cast with Carol Haney) was a failure, but Inge and Kazan still believed in Warren, and when *Splendor in the Grass* was ready for production in 1960, they cast Warren opposite Natalie Wood, who, although younger, was already a star because of such films as *Miracle on 34th Street* and *Rebel Without a Cause*.

Already, Warren had a reputation as a ladies' man, going out in his poverty stricken days in New York with a young actress, Diane Ladd, who was equally hard up and shared an apartment with three other women (one of whom was to gain fame as Hollywood gossip columnist Rona Barrett). Beatty dropped Ladd when he went to Hollywood to test for Logan, and soon was dating the beautiful English actress, Joan Collins.

One can see how Warren's reputation as a lover grew by what Collins says about him in her autobiography, *Past Imperfect*. While in New York with him during the rehearsals of *Roses*, she visited an actress friend who had been happily married for several years to a handsome superstar.

> "I don't think I can last much longer," I said, lighting a much needed cigarette—frowned upon by Warren.
> "He never *stops*—it must be all those vitamins he takes."
> She smiled warmly, dispensing coffee and sisterly advice. "Just like my husband," she said.
> "After all those years you've been together!" I said incredulously.
> "Oh yes. In fact it gets better."
> "Better—oh, God. Please." I leaned back and took a drag on the cigarette. "In a few years, I'll be worn out."
> "Take my advice, Joan," warned my friend. "Don't reject him. If you do, he may find it necessary to go with other women."

Collins's friend's advice would turn out to be absolutely correct. The relationship was in trouble, partially due to Joan's having to abort Warren's child, and partially due to his trying to take over her career, reading her scripts, and eventually persuading her not to make *Sons and Lovers*, which would have proved her acting ability. Instead she flew to Rome to make one of the worst, and unintentionally funniest, biblical epics in the history of film, *Esther and the King*. Warren stayed in New York to make *Splendor*, and though he was insanely jealous of Joan, the inevitable happened, and he began an affair with his co-star, Natalie Wood, who was then married to Robert Wagner.

As Warren had just proposed to Joan before she left for Rome and had given her an engagement ring, the rumors reaching her in Italy were upsetting. When she came back to the States, however, she and Warren seemed to settle down, and continued to live together in Hollywood. Then Joan got what might have been the biggest break of her career. Very early one morning, the phone rang and she was asked to come back to England immediately to replace Elizabeth Taylor in *Cleopatra*, because Elizabeth was desperately ill. As it turned out, Taylor survived, and it wasn't Joan, but Warren, who was called to London.

Warren had desperately wanted to play the role of the Italian gigolo, Paulo, in Tennessee Williams's *The Roman Spring of Mrs. Stone*. Warner Brothers didn't feel he was right to play opposite Vivien Leigh, so Warren sought out Williams who was vacationing in Puerto Rico to convince the playwright. Putting on a shiny Italian suit and wearing olive-tinted makeup, Warren approached Williams in a casino with a glass of milk on a tray (having heard that Williams was suffering from ulcers), and began to speak to him with an Italian accent. He got Williams to agree to hear him read for the part, and Williams seemed to like him. But Warren wasn't sure and, according to Williams, that night came to his bedroom dressed in a bathrobe. Williams said, "Go home to bed, Warren. I said you had the part."

Warren flew to London to work with one of the most beautiful actresses of all time, Vivien Leigh, who, at forty-eight, was in the middle of a divorce from Sir Laurence Olivier, who had fallen in love with the actress Joan Plowright. Vivien Leigh was beginning to suffer from the mental instability that made a travesty of the last few years of the life of the wonderful woman who captured the heart of the world as Scarlett O'Hara in *Gone With the Wind*. Although she was a shadow of her former self, Warren was not above having an affair with her while they were filming. It was this that led Joan Collins finally to decide to end their relationship.

Warren went back to Natalie Wood, living with her after she divorced Robert Wagner, as he had no home of his own, preferring to live out of one suitcase in a hotel room. While he was with Natalie he also put the make on her younger sister, Lana. He and Natalie were offered *Barefoot in the Park*, but he turned it down. Next he turned down *PT 109*, the story of John F. Kennedy's wartime exploits, and then he turned down the opportunity to play what became the Alain Delon role in Luchino Visconti's masterpiece, *The Leopard*.

Warren had made only three films; none had been critical or box-office successes. Finally he agreed to make *Lilith*, in which he gave a decent performance, although he argued with director Robert Rossen continually. The film wasn't a success, though it seems that Beatty was able to carve another notch in his belt in the person of his co-star, Jean Seberg.

His next film was a minor classic, *Mickey One*, directed by Arthur Penn, with whom he did get along. Then came *Promise Her Anything*, in 1965. Two years before, Warren had been introduced to Leslie Caron by her agent Freddie Fields (who was later to work so closely with Diane), when he gave a party to celebrate her Oscar nomination for *The L-Shaped Room*. Warren immediately fell for this beguiling French actress, the star of such classics as *An American in Paris*, *Lili*, and *Gigi*. She was six years older than he, but after that introduction they never left each other's side. Caron was the wife of one of the most distinguished directors in the English theater, Peter Hall, and the mother of their two children. But she was besotted with Beatty, and stayed in America for the next year to be with him and fulfill her film commitments. Eighteen months later Hall filed for divorce, naming Beatty as co-respondent. Beatty had to pay the court costs of the case, which was a major scandal in England.

Under the terms of the divorce, Caron could not take her children out of England, so Warren moved to London with her. It was there that he made two rather bad films, *Promise Her Anything*, with Caron, and *Kaleidoscope*, with Susannah York.

While obviously enjoying the fleshpots of the "Swinging London" of the sixties, he knew that he was wasting his time in films like these. He loved Caron very much and wanted to marry her, and it was she who would, in effect, make his career.

On a trip to Paris Caron introduced Warren to the French director, François Truffaut. At lunch together, Truffaut told Warren about a script he had received by two young writers at *Esquire* magazine, David Newman and Robert Benton. It was the story of two Texas outlaws, Bonnie Parker and Clyde Barrow. Truffaut couldn't make the film and suggested it would be an ideal vehicle for Beatty and Caron.

Beatty returned to the States, purchased the rights from Benton for $10,000, and the rest, as they say, is movie history. Warren asked Arthur Penn to direct, and after Newman and Benton had taken out the homosexual aspect of the story— Clyde's impotence and love for his sidekick, C.W. Moss, which fascinated Warren—Warner Brothers agreed to finance it. Warren, ruthless as ever over his career, then called Caron to Hollywood to tell her she wasn't right for the part. After a long search, he found an unknown young actress called Faye Dunaway to play Bonnie Parker.

This put an end to any feelings Caron had for Warren, but he was off and rolling. The film was shot quickly and cheaply, for which much credit has to be given to Beatty, who proved to be a brilliant producer. And even though he proved to be a perfectionist about every detail, including having just the right peach flown in for one scene when they were out of season in Texas, he pulled the movie in under budget. However, Jack Warner didn't like the film, considering it too violent, and Warren had to reduce his fee, in the process getting a greater percentage of the gross receipts, to get it exhibited. Warners finally agreed to distribute the film, but did nothing to promote it, showing it in only two New York theaters in the middle of August (a traditionally slow period).

The reviews were mixed, and Warners felt justified that they forced Beatty to finance the film virtually by himself. Then something started to happen. Word got around and the weekly receipts began to grow; certain major critics wrote second articles, reevaluating their earlier opinions. The film was also a major hit in London. Warren forced Warners to give it a wider release here, and then *Bonnie and Clyde* was nominated for ten Oscars. At the end of its first year, *Bonnie and Clyde* had grossed over $30 million, making Warren one of the richest young men in Hollywood.

While *Bonnie and Clyde* proved that Warren had an astounding talent in one respect, in many ways his career has been one of lost opportunities. He turned down such films as *Ryan's Daughter*, *Butch Cassidy and the Sundance Kid*, *The Way We Were*, *Last Tango in Paris*, *The Sting*, and *The Godfather* (the role of Michael Corleone, played by Al Pacino). Many of these films were the hottest properties of their time, and with hindsight it's hard to understand why he refused them. Looking back, it's almost as though Warren were acting as a single-man employment agency for Robert Redford, who benefited so much from Warren's lack of judgment. Indeed, Warren turned down *The Great Gatsby*, which gave Redford yet another plum part. While Warren's choice of other films for himself during the early seventies seems so misguided, he did give a wonderful performance in *McCabe and Mrs. Miller*, during which he met the Oscar-winning English actress Julie Christie, who was to become one of his great loves.

Warren created his next two productions for her. The first was *Shampoo*, a bitingly real parody of sexuality and politics in Bel Air set in 1968. Directed by Hal Ashby from Warren's first screenplay, which he co-wrote with Robert Towne, it was one of the best films of the early seventies. Warren played a hyper-heterosexual hairdresser in Beverly Hills, who goes to bed with anything female that walks upright on two legs. With a superb cast that included Goldie Hawn, Lee Grant, Jack Warden, and, of course, Julie Christie, it's a very special satire that gets better with viewing now.

Warren is slow to bring his films to a conclusion, and it wasn't

until three years later that he made *Heaven Can Wait*, a remake
of the 1941 classic *Here Comes Mr. Jordan*, about a boxer who
dies before he's supposed to, and comes back in another person's
body to finish what he has to do on earth. The role was transposed to a football player—a vanity of Beatty's, remembering
his school days. He paid $25,000 for the rights to the film, and
co-scripted it with Elaine May. Warren had originally asked Peter Bogdanovitch to direct but finally decided to co-direct it
himself with veteran director Buck Henry.

It was the first time since *Citizen Kane* that anyone had dared
to produce, direct, write, and star in a single film, and it shows
how powerful and respected Warren had become in the Hollywood community. Again with a marvelous cast, including
James Mason, Jack Warden, Charles Grodin, Dyan Cannon,
and Buck Henry (also acting), as well as Julie Christie, *Heaven
Can Wait* was a triumph for Warren. He was nominated for Best
Actor, Best Film, Best Screenplay, and Best Director.

At forty-one, in prime condition for his role as a football
player, Warren looked outstanding, as the movie poster, photographed by Michael Childers, with Warren in a track suit sport-
ing wings, will attest. It was at the Academy Award ceremony
in which he had four nominations, in March 1979, that his sister, Shirley, publicly made fun of him in front of a world television audience and in front of his new love, Diane Keaton.

When Diane and Warren first fell in love is difficult to ascertain, but it was most likely in the early summer of 1978. Up to
that point Warren was busy putting the finishing touches on
Heaven Can Wait, and Diane was in between filming two of
Woody's best films; *Interiors* and *Manhattan*.

Interiors opened in the beginning of August 1978, a scant
month after Warren's *Heaven Can Wait*. Woody's first "serious"
film was received by the critics with some shock. While everyone admired it, not everyone was convinced by the unrelenting
pace and message of the film. *Variety* called it "downbeat and
somber," Canby in *The New York Times* admitted he didn't like

the film, but praised Woody for his bravery in making it, writing, "These aren't laughing matters. How brave Mr. Allen is in taking them seriously. And how impressive he is in understanding them so well." But the importance of the film can be gauged by the fact that the *Times* devoted four separate articles to the film in its daily and Sunday editions.

Interiors was obviously controversial; Woody Allen should not make a film with no laughs was the consensus of his by now numerous devotees. Whether Woody was trying too hard with *Interiors*, or whether the public simply didn't want heavy drama that summer, they seemed very happy with Warren's *Heaven Can Wait*, which they were flocking to in droves. Undoubtedly, Woody's was the more thinking film, but to compare the two is unfair. When Woody was admired, it was without reservation. Critic Nora Sayre suggested that Woody's portrayal of the relationship between a mother and her daughters was a far better film that Bergman's own *Autumn Sonata*, which touched on the same subject, and came out around the same time. David Denby in *New York* magazine also suggested that Woody "outBergmaned Bergman." For an American "popular" filmmaker to be compared with one of the great geniuses of European cinema is praise enough.

Likewise, Diane's reviews for *Interiors* were mixed, but the majority considered it her finest performance to date. *Newsweek*, like many of the notices, praised all the performers, with Jack Kroll saying, "Jordan, Keaton and Page are excellent, especially Keaton and Page, who express and redeem alienation with their shading depth and humanity." Pauline Kael in *The New Yorker*, now an admirer, said, "This physical transformation [referring to Diane's less-than-glamorous appearance in the film] is the key to Keaton's performance: She plays an unlikable woman—a woman who dodges issues whenever she can." Penelope Gilliatt, in the same publication, was more forthright, saying that Diane gave "the performance of her career."

During the fall of 1978, Diane was most preoccupied with making what is considered Woody's best film ever, *Manhattan*.

Allen takes a long time to shoot his movies, between sixteen and twenty weeks (the norm is about nine or ten), so Diane had to be on call for at least four months, although she wasn't, in this film, required on the set every day. Film insurance companies prohibit principals to travel during shooting, so Warren would have had to come to New York to see Diane, rather than see her at his sparse Bauhaus-inspired house on Mulholland Drive.

Woody's new movie was a fable about his beloved New York, and the characters that make it so special. Taking another creative chance, *Manhattan*, possibly his most beautiful film, is photographed in black and white by Gordon Willis to a score of some of George Gershwin's most beautiful melodies, arranged and adapted by Tom Pierson. The film opens with the Manhattan skyline silhouetted at sunset. The anonymous monoliths that constitute the island's neo-Gothic outline, redolent of stalagmites, appear as beautiful pieces of sculpture when accompanied by the strains of Gershwin's *Rhapsody in Blue*. All the more indicative is that this title sequence is filmed from the terrace of Woody's Fifth Avenue penthouse.

Woody was back as his fans like him, playing the protagonist, Isaac Davis, in his own screenplay (co-written by Marshall Brickman). Davis is a successful TV comedy writer, who decides to quit his job to write a novel—not the great American novel, but a popular work of fiction about New York and the people around him. Meanwhile Davis's wife, Jill, who has left him for a woman, is writing a book about their marriage, telling the *whole* truth. It's called *Marriage, Divorce and Selfhood*, and it causes Davis much anguish. Since his wife left him, Davis has had an affair with an aspiring actress, Tracy, who's only seventeen years old. Somehow, due to the usual convoluted plots that Woody weaves, he then takes up with a know-it-all pseudo-intellectual, a sharp, successful literary journalist, Mary Wilke, a Radcliffe graduate, who's the girlfriend of his best friend, Yale, a married professor writing the definitive biography of Eugene

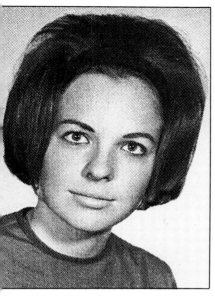

iane Hall, a senior in the class of 1963.
ourtesy of Santa Ana Senior High School

Diane as Carrie in *Carousel* at Santa Ana
College, 1963.
Courtesy of Bob Blaustone

In *Bye Bye Birdie* at Orange Coast College, 1964.
Courtesy of Orange Coast College

"Black Girls, White Girls." Diane, bottom center, in the cast of *Hair*, 1968.
Photofest

An early publicity still, 1971.
Barnard Nagler/Globe Photos

Diane was perceived as "Woody's Girl" during the early '70s, before she became recognized as one of America's most accomplished film actresses.
Adam Scull/Rangefinders Globe Photos

Woody Allen wears the famous "sneakers" with First Lady Betty Ford. What was less reported was Woody's date for the Martha Graham Benefit at Lincoln Center— a very chic Diane Keaton. New York 1975. *AP/Wide World Photos*

At the 46th annual Academy Awards in 1974 with Al Pacino.
Alpha Blair/Pictorial Parade

The first accolade for *Annie Hall*. Diane is chosen Best Actress by the New York Critics for her role as Annie.
AP/Wide World Photos

With fame, a new romance. Diane with Warren Beatty in one of their first public outings.
AP/Wide World Photos

Diane (holding her hairbrush) with her mother, father, and Warren, arriving at the Winter Garden Theater in New York to see *Forty-Second Street*. September 1980.
AP/Wide World Photos

Diane Keaton walking on Broadway,
summer 1988. *Vinnie Zeffante/Star File*

At the Cannes Film Festival in 1987,
Diane was very much the movie star!
Ducan Rabin/Globe Photos

The quintessential Diane Keaton,
in the role that made her a
superstar and fostered a whole
fashion look, Annie Hall.
Photofest

Diane's first try at comedy without Woody—and her first studio film—was a disaster. *I Will, I Will . . . For Now* did have its moments however. Here with Elliott Gould at a sex clinic.
Photofest

Her second film of 1976, *Harry and Walter Go to New York*, was slightly more successful. Diane's with Michael Caine.
Photofest

In her second film of 1977, Diane demonstrates that she's a dramatic film actress as well, in *Looking for Mr. Goodbar*.
Photofest

A very different role for Diane, as a terrorist in *The Little Drummer Girl*.
Photofest

Back in period costume again.
Diane in her critically
acclaimed role of Mrs. Soffel.
Photofest

Diane returns to comedy, and the
public flocks to see her again after
eight years of commercially not very
successful films. In *Baby Boom* she
proves she is still one of the cinema's
leading comediennes.
Photofest

O'Neill. Yale lends Mary to Davis, who's trying to get rid of Tracy, and so it goes . . .

The cast, with seventeen-year-old Mariel Hemingway as Tracy; one of Woody's best friends, Michael Murphy, as Yale; Meryl Streep as Jill; and Diane as Mary Wilke, was outstanding. To be able to see two of the best actresses on the screen in America today, Streep and Keaton, in the same film, by one of the best American filmmakers is quite amazing. *Manhattan* deserved every accolade the press and the public gave it.

To cite all the reviews would be superfluous: they all have the same message, only with different words. Indicative is that *Time* magazine gave Woody a cover because of *Manhattan*. Everyone was lauded, and Diane was singled out for her performance. Yet again we are told that Diane gave "her boldest, most interesting performance to date," to quote David Denby. One can gauge Diane's performances during this stage of her career by noting that each time her performance is cited as better than the last. What it denotes is an actress who has matured to such an extent that every time she walks on screen she is envisaged as better than before.

By the time *Manhattan* came out, at the end of April, 1979, Diane was already embroiled in Warren's great vision, the film he had been working toward for so many years, and the film he was finally able to make because he was so fascinated by Diane. It would take up most of the next two years of her life.

During the early months of 1979, however, Diane was more involved with a project far removed from the screen. For a long while she had been photographing the deserted lobbies of hotels across the country, from Florida to Los Angeles to New York to Las Vegas. Her photographs reflected the awful loneliness and decrepitude these public places present. Each image is different, although they are all joined by a feeling of wilderness. Diane said about her images, which were first shown at the Castelli Graphics Gallery on 57th Street in New York, "There's a certain mystery and tension and cheapness in these hotels. They're personal but impersonal. Lots of places kicked me out; they didn't want me taking pictures even when they knew who I was." This collection of photographs, published as a book, *Reservations*, in 1980, is very telling about Diane herself. More than the tackiness and sadness of exposed wires and bare bulbs, there is a feeling of limbo, akin to the Catholic concept of Purgatory, about her images. They're sad, but they are also full of incisive humor. They are not only a record of American hotels, but an insight into Diane's soul.

That Diane had been creating these images for several years is less important than the time she decided to publish them. They are bleak, they suggest loneliness, and that she had her exhibition during the high point of her affair with Warren makes one wonder if she was really happy even then.

They were obviously delighted in each other—one only has to see pictures of them together to realize that. Diane had gone so far as to buy a co-op in one of the most expensive buildings on Central Park West in New York, which must have set her back at least a million. Warren was engaged in bringing to realization the project that had engrossed him for nearly a decade—for her. All this suggests that Diane and Warren were hopelessly in love. But perhaps the indicative word is "hopelessly"—their feelings were doomed to failure because of their natures. Diane was too loyal and too strong to tolerate Warren's adolescent attitude toward women for long.

Perhaps he best expressed it himself, unknowingly, in his script for *Shampoo*. In the last scene of the film he gives himself this monologue:

Here Jill (Goldie Hawn), in the cold light of dawn, after revels and many infidelities on a November night in 1968, Election Day, tells her live-in lover George Roundy (Beatty), a promiscuous Beverly Hills hairdresser, that she is leaving him for another man. But before she goes she wants to know one last thing: How many women has he been unfaithful with while they were together?

GEORGE :   *(Sighs)* There were a couple . . . I mean there
(noises, sighs) . . . Let's face it, I mean, that's
what I do *(noises)*. That's why I went to beauty
school. I mean, they were always there and I
keep, I just, I, I, I *(noise)*. You know, I, I, I
don't know what I'm apologizing for *(sighs)*.
I go into that shop and they're looking so great,
you know. And I, I'm doing their hair, and
they feel great, and they smell great. Or I
could be out on the street, you know, and I
could just stop at a stoplight, or go into an elevator, or, I . . . there's a beautiful girl. I, I, I
don't know . . . I mean that's it. I— it makes
my day. Makes me feel like I'm gonna live forever. And, as far as I'm concerned, with what
I'd like to have done at this point in my life, I
know I should have accomplished more. But
I've got no regrets. I mean, gee, because . . . I
mean *(noises)* Aaagh! *(sighs)* Maybe that means I
don't love 'em. Maybe it means I don't love
you. I don't know. Nobody's going to tell me I
don't like 'em very much.

Is it George or is it Warren speaking? He collaborated on the
screenplay with his close friend Robert Towne, and judging by
Beatty's own predilection for casual sexual encounters with
women, it would seem that for once he let his famous guard down
and revealed more of himself than he's ever done in an interview.
He adores women, but he can be equally unconcerned and callous
toward them, especially when they interfere with his vision of his
work, as exemplified by his treament of Leslie Caron with *Bonnie
and Clyde*.

There's no doubt that Warren has the ability to bewitch
women. As Woody once quipped, when asked what he would
like to be if he came back to earth: "Warren's fingertips." Woody
would settle for that, just to have part of Warren's magnetism,

but Diane is too observant to be totally beguiled. For someone so apologetic and self-effacing, she still knows her own worth and talent when it comes to her profession. And while she admired Warren professionally, and loved him for himself, she wasn't about to sacrifice her self-esteem for his ego.

Perhaps David Thomson in his schizophrenic biography, *Warren Beatty and Desert Eyes*, put it best:

> Beatty may see in Keaton not just the realization of his sense of Louise Bryant, John Reed's wife, but the living woman. And Keaton is very far from just the best available actress for this central role, she is a shy but assertive woman, a good photographer (someone with her own work) who will display a cool ironic sensibility in *Reservations* (a study of hotel lobbies) and *Still Life*, her droll collection of old Hollywood production stills. No other Beatty film contains so large or troubling a portrait of a woman, or is so concerned with sexual politics. And Diane Keaton deserves credit for that, not simply as a performer but as a generating influence, the voice and independence Beatty hears the most.

Thomson, perhaps not realizing what he was doing, has perhaps given the most succinct analysis of Warren and Diane's relationship. While maybe not entirely as self-confident as she should be given her stage and screen portrayals, Diane is undoubtedly a woman of tremendous inner strength and conviction. For once, while not decrying the fortitude of his other "leading ladies," Warren had finally met his match!

But it was not Beatty's philandering that destroyed their relationship: what destroyed it was one of the most ambitious projects in the history of the movies.

REDS

Political radical and journalist John Reed, the only American to be buried in the Kremlin along with the esteemed members of the Communist oligarchy, had been the object of Beatty's studious research since at least 1972, when he filmed the first (though never used) of the interviews that distinguished his flawed masterpiece, *Reds*, in its final form.

In 1976, Beatty, continuing to turn down some of the most sought-after roles in American cinema, finally decided to commit himself to this pet project. Traveling by car with English playwright Trevor Griffiths to director Mike Nichols's wedding in Connecticut, the seeds were sown, and a week later Warren called Griffiths and asked what he knew about Reed.

"What do you want to know?" Griffiths replied.

"I don't want to know anything," said Warren in his usual truculent manner. "I've been looking at the guy's life for the last ten years."

After eight months' worth of transatlantic calls on the telephone Warren uses so compulsively, Beatty commissioned Griffiths to write a script about Reed. Then indeed he found out that Warren had been looking into Reed's life. Visiting the

Widener Library at Harvard to study Reed memorabilia (Reed was a Harvard graduate), the first loan card Griffiths found on research of the subject was made out to Warren Beatty, predating his inquiry by ten years. Griffiths's finished work, *Comrades*, while not yet entirely what Warren was looking for, was presented to Barry Diller, chairman of Paramount Pictures, who agreed to make the movie.

The script was so weighty and unwieldy that Diller knew it was going to be an extremely expensive project. Diller could not justify a final go-ahead without the approval of the late Charles Bluhdorn, chairman until his death in 1983 of Gulf and Western, Paramount's parent company, so he set up an appointment with Beatty and Bluhdorn in New York, adding that the script must be edited for this vital meeting.

In the next few days, in one of those spurts of energy that Beatty is so capable of despite his lackadaisical attitude, he, Elaine May (whom he had hired to write the screenplay of *Heaven Can Wait*, which he eventually co-wrote with her), and several others sat down to cut the script. The result, from too much hurrying, was a mess; yet Beatty's breakfast meeting with Bluhdorn couldn't be postponed without severely damaging *Comrades'* chance of "getting in the can." Legend has it that Beatty, in one of the finest gambles of his out-on-a-limb career, took a copy of the *Heaven Can Wait* script and put it between the covers of his new title for the project, *Reds*.

One can imagine Warren, acting his modest best, saying to Bluhdorn, in words his biographer David Thomson gave him, "I know you don't have time to *read* this, Charlie." Elaine May would be strategically placed at a nearby table in the Hotel Carlyle restaurant to cause a diversion just in case Bluhdorn decided to do just that! Whether this story is real or apocryphal, whatever Beatty actually did worked: Paramount decided to go ahead with *Reds*.

Work on the screenplay continued, with May as well as, reportedly, Robert Towne and Robert Benton, among others, being brought in to help. According to actress Coral Browne,

Beatty was also consulting late at night with writer Lillian Hellman about the radical movement in America. From the subterfuge, with Hellman trying to keep these visits secret from her house guest Browne, one can sense that Beatty was even more paranoid than usual. In fact there never was a final version of the screenplay. During the filming only Keaton and Jack Nicholson had a script, and even their versions were far from the final screenplay. Eventually Beatty gave the actors their lines just before they were to shoot a scene: Keaton, trying to reassure other actors on the set would say, "Don't worry. It doesn't matter. It's all in Warren's head anyway. He keeps changing it all the time." It may have been in his head but on a movie of this size that was a passport to disaster.

Yet the project rumbled relentlessly forward. In March 1979, Beatty, Keaton, production designer Richard Sylbert, and cinematographer Vittorio Storaro, went to Russia to scout locations. The question was whether the Soviets would allow Beatty, the epitome of American capitalism, to film in Leningrad or not. After endless meetings and banquet after banquet, with the inevitable vodka and numerous and heady toasts (Warren's was usually a rather cynical, "Let us drink to an end of bureaucracy"), the Russians came to the point. They asked, to see a script. Beatty, true to form, refused. So Russia, as a backdrop to this film about the revolution, was out. Beatty settled for Helsinki, some of whose buildings had been designed by the same Italian architect, Bartolomeo Rastrelli, who was brought to Russia by Empress Catherine the Great to rebuild and beautify St. Petersburg (Petrograd, or, as it is now called, Leningrad).

Shooting began in August 1979 and went on until July 1980. The mammoth crew was transported from Helsinki to London, to New York, to Washington, to Spain and back again. John Reed may have written *Ten Days that Shook the World*, but *Reds* was going to become the 240 days that shook Paramount. The budget, originally slated for $20 million, would grow and grow. Paramount's official estimate is currently "over $40 million," which probably means the film cost in the region of $50 million.

In order to make a profit, *Reds* would have to earn $125 million at the box office. Paramount was getting worried, would this be their version of *Cleopatra* or *Camelot*, which nearly ruined Twentieth Century Fox and Warner Brothers, respectively, in the sixties? It was not an unreal fear, after all, Michael Cimino's *Heaven's Gate*, concurrently being filmed for United Artists, would bring the company founded by Mary Pickford, Douglas Fairbanks, Charlie Chaplin, and D.W. Griffith to financial ruin. TransAmerica then divested itself of UA, with the result that it became part of MGM, and has now ceased to exist as a separate entity. That UA then had many successful money makers, such as the Bond, Pink Panther, and Rocky series, as well as (ironically) Woody Allen's continuing output, demonstrates how devastating a runaway production can be to a major film company. (Although admittedly UA was reeling at the same time from the cost of Francis Ford Coppola's *Apocalypse Now*, another wildly extravagant enterprise from one of Hollywood's *auteurs*.)

Hollywood is a very tight-knit community, and during the second half of 1979 and the beginning of 1980 rumors were flying about the excesses of both *Heaven's Gate* and *Reds*. The former's budget was, according to Steven Bach in his book *Final Cut*, originally slated for $7.5 million and finally settled at $11,588,000; far less than Beatty's $20 million for *Reds*, but the cost of both productions was escalating in a similar way. Both directors had demanded closed sets (Beatty's cousin David McLeod, associate producer of the film, spent most of his time trying to keep the media away rather than providing them with information), but stories began to leak out about excesses on both films. Not only were there the "necessary" costs of thousands of extras and costumes but *Variety* (the movie trade paper) in an article on *Reds* in its March 26, 1980, issue cited such overhead items as rewrites, crew overtime, actors being flown to England, Spain, and Scandinavia to deliver a couple of lines, as well as a shooting ratio of thirty-five takes to the one used, compared to an average of between five and ten takes. The film crew was sent to a location only sixty miles outside London on

British Rail in first class, while Beatty and Nicholson flew down by helicopter! The money-wise attention to detail that Beatty had demonstrated while producing *Bonnie and Clyde*, *Shampoo*, and *Heaven Can Wait* seemed to have evaporated.

The stories about *Heaven's Gate* are even more scandalous. As early as one week into the sixty-nine-day shooting schedule, and having exposed 60,000 feet of film, Cimino was five days behind schedule and had only about a minute and a half of usable material, which had cost UA approximately $900,000 to expose. The shooting ratio was somewhere in the region of 50:1. Cimino was even trying to get away with making the studio pay for an irrigation system for the land he had secretly bought in Montana by insisting it was the only perfect location for the final battle scene in the movie. He maintained that the grass should be green for this one and a half hour sequence! (Even Cimino's lawyer told UA executives that this was "less than appropriate," and Cimino had to agree not to shoot the one and a half hour battle scene on his own land.)

Certainly Beatty wasn't trying to cheat Paramount in this way, but the parallels are obvious between the two productions. In an attempt to quell the rumors, Michael Eisner, then president of Paramount, issued this statement: "I certainly don't consider it a project that's out of control." In defining an out-of-control production, Eisner said it was, "one of those pictures that go two hundred to four hundred percent over budget today, and *Reds* is nothing like that. It isn't a situation like *The Blues Brothers* or *1941*. Warren is a responsible filmmaker who's going over schedule with responsibility by about fifteen to twenty percent."

Somehow an escalation from $20 million to somewhere around $50 million isn't fifteen or twenty percent, but Paramount was closing ranks. Whatever Paramount might have stated publicly, a certain desperation undoubtedly existed at the Gulf and Western building on Columbus Circle and at 5451 Marathon Street (Paramount's East and West Coast headquarters) over the costs that were rising on an exponential curve for a film that still had no final script. And this was perhaps the biggest problem.

The complexity and cost of the production can be imagined by considering the logistics. Actors were being flown back and forth from New York and Hollywood to London. Writers like Elaine May, in desperate attempts to get a working script (while the film was actually in production) were also being transported. Crowd scenes were scheduled the likes of which hadn't been seen since the Hollywood epics of the fifties and sixties. Accurate period props such as trains, cars, and costumes were needed, as well as locations that would not be anachronistic. In England alone the Reeds' Croton-on-Hudson house was found in Kent, the Provincetown beach at Camber Sands in Lincolnshire, as well as locations around Manchester; the interiors were shot at Twickenham Studios in England. Beatty had agreed to pay Screen Actors Guild rates, which were higher than British Actors Equity rates, and the British unions had insisted that a full English camera crew stand by because cinematographer Vittorio Storaro had insisted on having his own Italian crew.

No wonder Barry Diller was worried about the production. As he later candidly explained to writer Aaron Latham, in his insightful analysis of Beatty and *Reds* in *Rolling Stone:*

> Producing *Reds* was misunderstood by all of us. It was miscalculated. What happened was that no preproduction work was done on the film; we had to start immediately because of the availability of the actors. So it was always catch-up. It was originally budgeted at $20 million. It should have been budgeted in the high twenties or low thirties. I got very frustrated, because the film was clearly going to cost vastly more than contemplated. My knee-jerk reaction was to get angry with Warren. At the worst stage, I just refused to talk to him. I thought that would have some effect. That was naïve. Hurtful. Cruel. My behavior was unfortunate.

Diller's behavior was unfortunate. From shortly after the start of shooting in August 1980 until Thanksgiving he refused to talk to Warren, who was constantly calling him in New York or in Hollywood. It put more pressure on the writer-director-producer-star who knew, deep down, that *Reds* had problems. Diller's Thanksgiving visit was akin to an ultimatum: Get the production on schedule.

Diller visited London again just before Christmas and by that time Beatty had five hours of film to show him. Diller was pleased with what he saw and agreed to let Beatty continue the production. There was little he could do. By that time Paramount had spent too much money on *Reds* for them to back out. (Just like UA with *Heaven's Gate;* executives of the company liked what Cimino was coming up with, even though it was costing them a fortune.) Hence Eisner's public statement in January 1980 was issued, stating Paramount's support for the film that Hollywood wags were saying made the Russian Revolution look like a bargain.

Warren was doing everything to ensure the film would be the masterpiece he dreamed of. It was the first time he single-handedly took on every role he could play, apart from the co-writing of the screenplay with Griffiths (with help from a lot of people). It was the first time he would have single credits as producer and director. In *Heaven Can Wait* he shared the direction with Buck Henry, and in *Bonnie and Clyde* he produced, with Arthur Penn as director. There is no doubt the jobs were too much for him to handle, especially with what was virtually an unfinished script, even though he had the back-up of some of the best names in the business: Dede Allen as editor and executive producer, Richard Sylbert as designer, Vittorio Storaro as cinematographer, Shirley Russell for costumes, and Stephen Sondheim and Dave Grusin as composers.

The cast, besides Diane, included Jack Nicholson, Edward Herrmann, Paul Sorvino, Maureen Stapleton, Gene Hackman, writers George Plimpton and Jerzy Kosinski, and Keaton's close

friend, Kathryn Grody. It was a formidable list, with Oscar
winners abounding. So why didn't it work?

The script problems had a lot to do with it. As Sylbert later
said, "And you know, all the time we were learning—you
couldn't figure out how to do this picture unless you just started
doing it." There was also Warren's identification with the character he was playing. This is central to Beatty's acting process,
but here, as producer, it got him into trouble. One ridiculous
situation is recounted when, during a 110-degree heat wave in
Seville (southern Spain was cast as Baku in Russia), Beatty, not
well with flu and fatigue, explained through an interpreter to
the hundreds of Spanish extras what the scene was about. He
declaimed for over an hour explaining Reed's beliefs about the
working man being exploited by capitalists and why they
should rise up. At the end of his speech Beatty called for a
lunch break, while a disgruntled camera crew was strengthening
a podium that Warren felt wasn't strong enough. During this
break the extras came to Beatty and suggested that *they* were
being exploited and demanded a pay rise from $70 to $90 for the
day! Beatty acceded.

Since the film was costing over $50,000 a day to shoot an
extra $20 a day for an extra may not seem like much, but not
with hundreds of them. It was symptomatic of what was happening on the set of *Reds*. By this time his many roles were
taking their toll on Beatty. As Jerzy Kosinski recalls about this
period, Warren was living in a little hut with no hot water, a
hotplate to cook on, and a bathroom with a door that wouldn't
close. "I was living with him the last three months. He dressed
like John Reed onstage and off. He was in worse shape than
Reed. Exhausted. Coughing all the time. Sick. Emaciated."

But, according to insiders, there was something even more
disturbing happening.

Even as early as London, Warren and Diane took separate
houses, and certainly by the end Beatty was sharing his shack
with Kosinski. The two stars and lovers weren't even talking,
and their scenes together were fraught with tension.

Keaton, that consummate professional, was being asked to do up to forty takes for every scene. "Diane almost got broken," says George Plimpton. "I thought he [Beatty] was trying to break her into what Louise Bryant had been like with Reed."

. Later Jerzy Kosinski showed writer Aaron Latham the photo album he has made of the filming of the movie; in many, many of those photographs a very angry Keaton is captured arguing with a scowling Beatty in front of the camera. "It was not easy directing Diane," says Kosinski. Yet she had never been criticized as a difficult actress before (and hasn't been since), and in this case it was most likely the director's fault. This is borne out by problems Beatty had with some of his other actors.

Not only was Keaton under tremendous strain from Beatty's maniacal way of working, but so was Maureen Stapleton, one of America's most accomplished actresses. Playing the role of activist Emma Goldman, for which she won the Oscar, she turned on the director one day, after yet another of his demands of "Do it again," and sharply said, "No."

"Do it again," Beatty replied.

"What do you want me to do? Take off my clothes?" Stapleton retorted.

Wearily, Beatty said, "I don't know. Do it again." Beatty was obviously lost. In another scene with Stapleton, where the Goldman character is addressing a group of workers in a driving rainstorm, Beatty kept repeating, "Do it again." Finally after the umpteenth take he said, "Great." The cast, the crew, everyone, gave a sigh of relief . . . then, quietly, Beatty said, "One more time."

Stapleton, her considerable patience exhausted, shouted, "Are you out of your fucking mind?"

Everyone on the set burst into applause.

Warren's obsession and lack of objective control was affecting everybody involved with *Reds.* Yet, Diane, who was closest to him, suffered most. With the added pressure of having to fight her director and co-star professionally, it's obvious that their personal relationship suffered.

The rift between them artistically and professionally was deep, causing problems for the film Warren was making for himself, but perhaps also partially for his lover.

It's not coincidental that the films Beatty has produced have been for, or intended for, his girlfriend of the time—*Bonnie and Clyde* was originally intended as a vehicle for Leslie Caron, and *Shampoo* and *Heaven Can Wait* were for Julie Christie. There is often this symbiosis between Warren's private life and his film career; many of his leading ladies became or were his lovers. It's part of his adolescent charm that Warren, even though forty-three years old at the time of *Reds*, presented this film (as he had the others), like a puppy to his lovers. (Although, as in the case of Caron and *Bonnie and Clyde*, he was never afraid to ditch them if they didn't fulfill his artistic vision.)

On *Reds*, however, Warren, true to his libido, was not above playing around with other women, however much this could damage the delicate balance he was trying to achieve in the relationship between Reed and Bryant on camera. There is a story that soon after the crew arrived in Finland at the beginning of 1980, Beatty was taken up to see the location, one hundred miles above the Arctic Circle, of a railway station that he had had built. Out of the snow approached two figures. One of them said, "Warren, is that you, Warren?" It was a girl he had met previously at the Cannes Film Festival. Given that she had made her way to far north of the Arctic Circle, she wasn't one of Warren's ordinary camp followers.

Rising above all this, and however great their professional differences and personal problems were on *Reds*, Keaton's performance as Louise Bryant was one of the best things she had done to date.

By the end of July 1980 the whole inexorable edifice of moviemaking that Beatty had overseen like a general for the past year was dismantled. The actors, camera crews, sound engineers, lighting technicians, stunt persons, set builders, and props and wardrobe people, let alone the gofers, dressers, transport crews, and the rest of the pawns in the campaign that

Beatty waged to immortalize his vision of the Russian Revolution were dismissed. All that was left was the small crew Beatty and Storaro required to film the relics of the radical movement in New York with which Beatty so powerfully punctuates his "masterpiece." In the film thirty-two witnesses are quoted, but many more were filmed, some for as long as two hours.

On December 31, 1980, Army Archerd in his column for *Daily Variety* opened with:

> Happy New Year: And it must be a happy day at Paramount, now that Warren Beatty has wound up photography on *Reds* . . .

It couldn't have been so joyful at Paramount; *Reds*, like UA's cinematic Tower of Babel, *Heaven's Gate*, had been scheduled for a Christmas (in time for Oscar nomination) 1980 release.

In January 1981, Beatty, with the editing crew headed by the brilliant Dede Allen (who had edited his *Bonnie and Clyde* among other great films) and Craig McKay started to assemble the one-hundred-and-thirty hours of film Warren had shot and edit it down to a cohesive story that would play in the theaters. Beatty's professionalism was demonstrated in that the first cut was down to 220 minutes, and only twenty-one minutes would have to be cut from that for the release time of three hours and nineteen minutes. Though it was still long for a release, it was far less than Cimino's five and a half hour *Heaven's Gate* (which was later cut down to three hours and thirty-nine minutes, but without Mr. Cimino's editing; he lost that right under threat of being fired from his own film).

The editing of *Reds* was carried out at JRS Productions, the cutting rooms on West 54th Street, where so many of the most important films of the past decade have been brought to a conclusion, unbeknownst to the devotees of that artificial disco paradise, Studio 54, which was right next door.

Beatty, true to form, was everywhere, overseeing the editing to the point where he actually slept in the cutting room. By

September of that year a trailer of four and a half minutes was played in the theaters, even though Paramount hadn't yet seen the film. Paramount was desperately worried; the long trailer had been booed by audiences; so the studio decided to change tactics. They released an advance poster of Reed and Bryant embracing in the final scene from the film in an effort to promote the love theme, against Beatty's wishes. (Apparently Diane did have some say in it; it was her wish that her face not be seen in the poster.)

Finally, sometime in October, according to most sources (though *Film Journal* says it was as early as July, which is doubtful given the scenario of events), Beatty screened the film—still not finalized—for Diller and Bluhdorn. Both Diller and Beatty were worried what Bluhdorn, an immigrant who passionately believes in the American dream, would think about a story of American radicals and anarchists and the Russian Revolution, which he had financed to the tune of about a quarter of a million dollars for every screen minute. "It was a very emotional screening," said Diller later. "We could have brought shame and degradation on the company. We badly, emotionally, wanted him to say he approved." (It is interesting that in this statement Diller unconsciously admits how vital *Reds* was to Paramount's future—something company spokespeople never do in public.) The three men sat talking over dinner on the thirtieth floor of the Gulf and Western headquarters till after one in the morning. Luckily Bluhdorn loved Beatty's performance and especially loved Keaton's performance. The film was safe.

Next Beatty screened the film for Paramount's heads of distribution and marketing, Frank Mancuso and Gordon Weaver. They, while agreeing they had something special, were still worried, and not without cause. Not only was the subject of doubtful appeal but the length of the film meant that it would only get three or at the most four screenings a day, thereby losing revenue.

Also, *Reds* was given an *R* rating by the Motion Picture Association of America. This would cut down the chances of breaking even by a considerable amount, as it meant losing the whole of the youth market, the biggest attendees of movies in America today. Beatty, who had veto power over every aspect of the film attended the appeal before the review board with Mancuso, and even though Beatty refused to moderate or edit the language and the love scenes (and, according to one source, a "four-letter word" in Henry Miller's "witness" interview, to which the board stupidly reacted). His claim that the film merited *PG* rating due to its historical subject matter won the appeal. On November 19, fifteen days before its opening, the MPAA agreed. So far Beatty had not lost his charm.

Yet even on this positive note and the enthusiastic response at screenings to exhibitors in the anti-blind bid states on November 18, which were delayed by Beatty for a week—most likely because he was still unsatisfied with the finished product—he failed to quell the unease felt by many of Paramount's top executives. (Blind-bidding is a practice whereby the film company sells a production sight unseen, generally with incentives. It is a practice outlawed in twenty-two states).

Mancuso was worried that anyone would care enough about American radicals of the beginning of the century to draw an audience, and was strongly suggesting that they should sell the movie as a love story (the famous Beatty-Keaton embrace poster that Warren never liked). Beatty, unhappy with their concept of how the film should be promoted and marketed—a subject he had proven astute with for *Bonnie and Clyde*—independently hired a political pollster, Patrick Caddell, to survey the advance attitude of the public on *Reds*. Caddell's findings were that the more people found out about the subject matter of *Reds* (not a topic akin to American popular mainstream thought) the more interested they would be in it. The pity is that they didn't take Caddell's advice. *Life*, for instance, had wanted to do a color feature on the film, but Beatty wouldn't give them an interview, so they canceled the idea. Advance exposure like that could have helped the public's comprehension of, and therefore interest in, the subject.

Paramount had to fight Beatty throughout that fall for a finished product. Gordon Weaver jokingly responded to a question by Janet Maslin in *The New York Times* on November 5 about whether Paramount had forbidden Beatty to oversee the making of the prints in Rome, by saying, "Of course he can go to Rome. I have his passport right here in my drawer—but of course he can go to Rome!" Underlying the flippancy, Paramount and Beatty were definitely at odds.

Yet the question of publicity was even more important. Losing a *Life* spread was no small thing, and Beatty's intractability was cause for concern. Without prepublicity it was doubtful, even given the star cast, that the public would be drawn to *Reds* despite the enthusiastic response by exhibitors.

Paramount, it should be said, had done a marvelous job earlier in the summer in the blind bids. In their bid letters to exhibitors, they (possibly prompted by Beatty) had made extraordinary demands. According to one report they had requested a $100,000 guarantee and specified a sixteen-week playing time with the usual 90-10 (theater distribution) split against weekly minimums. As a result *Reds* was perceived as *the* film of the Christmas season by exhibitors who accepted the blind bids. According to one source at Paramount, "The main concern with exhibitors [about *Reds*] wasn't with having a hit but with *missing* a hit." However, deep down, Paramount was still worried— quite rightly as it turned out—that it would ever see any return on its $50 million investment.

(Whose investment it was is subject for debate. The copyright was held by Barclays Bank, one of the five British clearing banks, under a division of the bank called Barclay's Mercantile Industrial Finance Ltd. A loophole in the tax laws of the United Kingdom enabled Barclays to write off the cost of the film in the first year, unlike the United States where it would have to be written off over five years, and apparently Barclays actually financed the film, "leasing" it to Paramount who had the distribution rights.)

Meanwhile, Beatty, having megalomaniacally dismissed the

press, decided there was only *one* review he needed for the film. Despite being an avid Democrat, he felt the single approval he needed to promote what was to him a historical masterpiece was to go directly to the *top*. Just as Reed went to Lenin for an imprimatur for *Ten Days*, Beatty arranged a private screening in the White House for the President of the United States—a fellow thespian—Ronald Reagan. While it's hard not to imagine the elderly president not dozing off for at least part of the three and a half hours, Reagan gave the imperial sign of favor that Beatty had been hoping for—although, like the President's policies for the U.S., he said he wished it could have a happy ending.

And that is *all* Beatty did.

Practically no advance screenings were held for the press and Beatty refused to give interviews. So on December 4, 1981, *Reds* opened simultaneously in three hundred theaters across the country, practically cold. Tactically it was a dreadful mistake, and not one of Paramount's making. When Warner Brothers tried to hide *Bonnie and Clyde*, a movie they hated, it was Beatty who almost single-handedly got the film rereleased and turned it into a blockbuster. With *Reds* it was as if he didn't care. Perhaps he was upset by the poster and Paramount's wish to handle the film as a love story, yet after consuming ten years of his life one would think he would have fought even harder for this special baby of his. Was it that he was simply too tired—or too proud?

Even the reviews of *Reds* were controversial. Of the two trade papers *Variety* liked it—"a courageous and uncompromising attempt"—but with reservations, while the *Hollywood Reporter* decided to run two reviews; Arthur Knight gave it a rave and Robert Osborne dismissed it. However, many of the most distinguished critics in the country were extremely enthusiastic about the film. Accolades such as "spectacular," a "literate, visually stunning epic," "truly epic in scope," abounded. Vincent Canby in *The New York Times* went so far as to say, "*Reds* is an extraordinary film, a big romantic adventure movie, the best since David Lean's *Lawrence of Arabia*, as well as a commercial movie with a rare sense of history." *Time* called it, "a big, smart movie, vastly ambitious and entertaining . . . it combines the majestic sweep of *Lawrence of Arabia* and *Dr. Zhivago* . . . with the rueful comedy and historical fatalism of *Citizen Kane*."

These are obvious comparisons. Lean's two films were astounding in scope and Beatty, with *Reds*, had done what no single person in Hollywood had—directing, co-writing, producing, and starring in a film—since the twenty-four-year-old Orson Welles made movie history with *Citizen Kane*, and created himself into a genius. Yet, however flattering the reviews, there was always a hint of dissatisfaction with *Reds*. Beatty had cribbed many of the techniques utilized by Lean's and Welles's masterpieces, from the grand sweep of story, to the focusing in on minutiae to make a point, to the device of "witness" interviews. And Beatty is not the genius that Lean and Welles were at their best. As Andrew Sarris, critic for the *Village Voice*, succinctly concluded in his generally favorable review, "Above all it lacks a touch of genius, a touch of folly, a sustained flight of fancy."

Reds, however much a triumph for Beatty (some reviews even compared him to David O. Selznick, the brilliant maverick producer of *Gone With the Wind*), is flawed. Sometimes, to audiences, excruciatingly flawed. The film is far too long and the problems with the script patently obvious. The liberal Beatty couldn't decide whether he was making an apologia for the left-wing movement in America, a statement about free love, or a love story set against a dramatic historical backdrop. While his efforts should be applauded, the film was neither one nor the other, though he should have stuck to the last—it worked for David Lean in *Dr. Zhivago*. Simply put, *Reds*, while it has brilliant moments, some of the best acting seen from many of the cast, and is visually stunning, is indecisive, ponderous, and unwieldy.

Despite these faults it's hard to explain some of the criticism that *Reds* received. Most critical of all was *The New Yorker*'s Pauline Kael who may well have, as many, disliked the movie, but in her review her insightful critic's pen seemed to have been filled with vitriol. Kael *hated* the film and lambasted everything in it. While Ms. Kael had some very good points to make—"It's because of the way *Reds* wavers and searches for what it's trying to say that it needs this length"—she also derided the performances, which had been almost universally acclaimed by other critics.

Jack Nicholson, Maureen Stapleton, Gene Hackman—in fact nearly every member of the cast was praised for his or her performance. Beatty was also, for his portrayal of Reed, though David Thomson in *Film Comment* suggested that Keaton was the force behind Beatty's performance: "Beatty is not the easiest actor to play with: he can be chilly and hidden on screen—not so much out of vanity as caution. Some actresses have wilted in his presence, but Keaton assaults him, reads him the riot act, mauls him until the actor-producer-director rediscovers his own charm."

Most of all it was Keaton whom the press admired most. Canby in the *Times* said, "But Diane Keaton is nothing less than splendid as Louise Bryant—beautiful, selfish, funny, and driven. It's the best work she has done to date." *Rolling Stone* agreed, "Keaton convinces us, as she never has before, that she can play a woman of backbone. . . ."

The Academy of Motion Picture Arts and Sciences agreed. Diane Keaton was nominated for Best Actress for her portrayal of Louise Bryant, and *Reds* was nominated for a total of twelve Academy Awards, more than any other film since *Who's Afraid of Virginia Woolf*, in 1966. Beatty's peers, and the peers of everyone involved in the film, came out solidly in support of his supreme effort. The other hot contender for 1981 was *On Golden Pond*, with ten nominations, perhaps in part for nostalgia value; it was the last screen performance of Henry Fonda and the last, to date, of Katharine Hepburn. The race was on.

Unfortunately, at the box office *Reds* hardly got out of the starting gate. In its first three weeks of release the sophisticated audience that Paramount was banking on failed to be drawn to the film. Interestingly, it then began to pick up and, for one brief shining week, *Reds* made the number one spot in revenue across the country—quite a feat given its single showing per evening. But even this could not begin to give Paramount (and Beatty) a profit. They would need box-office returns of at least $125 million to show that. By April, *Reds* had grossed only about $30 million, less than the negative cost of the film and certainly less than the overall cost which included an extra $8 million in advertising that Paramount had pumped into it. In that same month, the *New York Daily News* reported that *Reds* was doing "dismally," drawing an average audience of fifty-seven people per performance in ten Manhattan theaters. The blame has to be laid at the feet of Warren Beatty, who refused to publicize one of the most expensive films ever made.

Today, *Reds* has probably paid back the investment that Barclays Bank and Paramount put into it with video and TV sales, but financially it has to be considered a disaster.

To Warren this might not have mattered if *Reds* had won a great percentage of the Academy Awards it was up for (which would also have brought in increased interest and revenue at the box office). As it was, it gained only three Oscars: Maureen Stapleton for Best Supporting Actress, Vittorio Storaro for Cinematography, and Warren for Best Director. Beatty had been nominated for Best Actor, Original Screenplay, Producer (best film), and Director.

In 1981, Paramount was sitting pretty. With thirty-three nominations—more than any other studio—for *Reds*, *Atlantic City*, *Raiders of the Lost Ark*, and *Ragtime*. The first three were up for Best Picture, so Paramount was sure to win, unless *On Golden Pond* won the ultimate gold statuette. To everyone's surprise it was a little-known and inexpensive British film that won—*Chariots of Fire*, directed by Hugh Hudson, produced by David Putnam, and released by Warner Brothers.

As for *Reds*, Nicholson's portrayal of Eugene O'Neill lost out to Sir John Gielgud's butler in *Arthur*; *Heaven's Gate* got one Oscar for art direction; *Raiders* picked up the sound and editing awards. *Reds* lost out in most other categories to *Chariots*.

The Best Actor and Actress categories were, with Hollywood

as sentimental as it is, a foregone conclusion. Warren understandably lost to a dying Henry Fonda, and Diane, despite her brilliant portrayal of Louise Bryant, could not hope to beat Katharine Hepburn who, with this Oscar, became not only the most nominated actress of all time but the only actress to win four Academy Awards.

Unlike the last time Diane was nominated, her co-star and co-nominee escorted her. In the public view Warren and Diane were still very much "the couple." And from Warren's powerful and generous acknowledgment of her talents in his acceptance speech for Best Director—"Miss Keaton, I know that public expressions like this can be embarrassing to you and that my chances of speaking with you in private are at the moment excellent, but I do want to tell you that you make every director you work with look good . . . and I think what they're trying to tell me here tonight is that I'm no exception"—it's obvious that the tenderness and love they felt for each other was there. But despite this simultaneously public and private sentiment, *Reds* had taken its toll: Their romance was as dead as their film was at the box office.

9

ALONE AGAIN

Warren has often been quoted as saying, perhaps in defense of his philandering, "Let's change partners and dance" lifestyle, that "Whenever a relationship has ended the decision has never been mine. It's always the other person's. And no matter what happened, I've never felt very far apart from any of the women with whom I've been involved. Some feeling always remains."

Definitely, even after the harrowing experience of *Reds*, Diane still felt strongly about Warren. After all, he had, according to diarist Nigel Dempster of England's *Daily Mail*, proposed marriage to her twice during the filming of his cinematic ode to their relationship. He was the first lover in her life to do that, but did she want to follow in Joan Collins's and Leslie Caron's footsteps? And despite their furious artistic differences on the *Reds* sets, Diane still admired Warren's creativity and search for perfection as a filmmaker. As she later told Gene Siskel in the *Chicago Tribune*, "The scene in *Reds* where I finally see him in the train station after all those years he's been away is an example of his commitment. I think we shot that scene of us walking toward each other amid the crowd about thirty times. And I believe the last one is the one that's in the movie."

But Diane, despite her continuing, deep insecurities, had by now begun to recognize the fierce, determined independence that ran in her family, especially from her grandmother, Mary. The affair was over, partly because of their artistic differences, and perhaps partly because the very proud Warren couldn't countenance the disaster that *Reds* was in reality, therefore blaming the person nearest to him—Diane.

It's also more than possible that Diane was not about to continue playing second fiddle to Warren's compulsive womanizing. He wasn't exactly demure about being seen around town with Mary Tyler Moore, Hope Lange, and model Janice Dickinson. When you are in love with someone, however much they may profess their devotion, the feelings of possession and jealousy can reach the strangulation point if your partner is always with someone else. And Diane needed the reassurance that she was loved.

But she was strong enough to say enough's enough, and while diffident about many aspects of her life, Warren is probably right in his weak defense that she left him. Nonetheless, she was hurt, so she threw herself back into the one thing she *knew* she was good at, even if she self-critically never felt she had achieved her own high standards in it—her work.

There seems to be no doubt that she still loved Warren deeply, and though during the Academy Awards ceremony in March 1982 they were seen to be, in public, very much attached, but the affair was over with *Reds*. During the filming for her next movie it was obvious to everyone on the set that Diane was finished with Warren, even though it was painful for her.

Significantly, she had chosen the subject of the breakup of a marriage for this film, *Shoot the Moon*. She could identify with Bo Goldman's brilliant, bittersweet comedy on many levels. Her parents' marriage had entered a difficult stage, she had just rejected marriage herself, and, aged thirty-six, she was beginning to realize that her childbearing years were diminishing. And this was a film about children. British director Alan Parker, who had made his name with *Bugsy Malone*, *Midnight Express*, and *Fame*, had wanted Diane for the film for a long time, even before she made *Reds*, but she wouldn't commit herself. The first time they met, for lunch at the Algonquin Hotel, Diane fazed him by saying "I don't eat lunch, but I'll watch you." Even so Parker had a marvelous time, laughing at this truly funny woman. After she left he realized that they hadn't even discussed the script; Diane had avoided the issue by entertaining him with almost the whole story of her life. Finally, after several more serious meetings she did commit herself, although, as he says, "At the beginning of *Shoot the Moon* she was at the end of her tether, but put an incredible amount of work into the role even before we had the script finished. She's a very wary lady and it was not immediately easy to get close to her. So she started to write me beautiful letters, four or five pages long, about her understanding of the role. I would sit down and say, 'How dare that———actress tell us what to do.' Then we'd admit she had a point. There were fifteen or twenty facets of the character that came from what Diane offered us."

Even Bo Goldman, the Oscar-winning screenwriter of *One Flew Over the Cuckoo's Nest* and *Melvin and Howard*, was won over by her professionalism. His attitude went from scathing—"I wasn't thrilled about it. Annie Hall as the mother of four kids!"—to complete respect. "Her notes [on the script] were as good as any I've ever seen. Simple thoughts, always presented in the most matter-of-fact, practical way. I often feel like a failed playwright, but Diane makes me feel good about writing for movies."

The critics, too, lauded her performance as Faith Dunlap, the wife of a writer, whose thirteen-year marriage is collapsing. She has to deal with her four children, especially the eldest, a thirteen-year-old who realizes Faith's situation and hates her father, George (played by Albert Finney), a successful novelist who has turned to another woman. Faith, in her turn, seduces the young man building a tennis court on the grounds of their large home in Marin County, just outside San Francisco. Ironically, many critics remarked on how tired Diane looked in the film, which they thought a courageous depiction of the role, but which was probably a more significant indication of how much the breakup with Warren had taken out of her. Though always there is that steely professionalism that exists in Diane, which means that she *decides* how she will look in a film. In this she was aided by the costume designer, Kristi Zea, who'd worked with her on Woody's *Interiors*, and therefore knew her style.

What was new for Diane in *Shoot the Moon* was the experience of playing a mother. She interacted with the children to a remarkable degree, especially the young actress Dana Hill, who played Sherry, the thirteen-year-old daughter most affected by her parents' breakup. As is said, "out of the mouths of babes," or in this case sensitive pubescent children, it was Dana who realized how hurt Diane was by the breakup with Warren. The crew, joking around as film crews always do, would continually ask Diane how the "Big W," Warren, was. Diane would simply walk away without answering, but one day Dana found her in her trailer crying her eyes out. In Dana's estimation it wasn't simply the end of her love affair with Warren, but that "the movie reminded her that she doesn't have that much longer to have kids." What Dana had instinctively realized was that Warren's proposals of marriage to Diane had subconsciously brought out her feelings of motherhood. As Diane was to tell the London *Sunday Times* shortly thereafter, "That's not something I knew until recently. I didn't even address myself to that. Now I have to because it's just so late."

When *Shoot the Moon* came out in January 1982, the critics, while divided about the film, were almost unanimously enthusiastic about Diane's performance. Indeed there was talk about an "Oscar performance" from her (which, given the Hollywood rumor mill, was one reason why many of her peers felt more than justified in awarding the Best Actress Oscar for 1981 to

Katharine Hepburn for sentimental reasons, as they felt sure Diane would win for 1982).

Unfortunately, however well she acted in *Shoot The Moon*, it wasn't quite enough to overcome the appeal of the fine performances in *An Unmarried Woman*, *Kramer vs. Kramer*, and *Ordinary People* in 1982, even though Stephen Schaefer in *US* magazine felt, "Keaton gives the performance of a lifetime. You can't imagine any actress getting better than this," and even Diane's critical nemesis, Pauline Kael, wrote, "Diane Keaton and Albert Finney give the kind of performances that in the theater become legend."

The year of 1981 was the beginning of a five-year period of soul searching for Diane. Her private life in tatters, she began to question what she really wanted from life. Even her collages from this period suggest this, with such inscriptions as, "ENVY: There is no greater torment" "NARCISSISM: Over-concern and preoccupation with one's own body, combined with exaggerated or abnormal sexual tendencies." Was she expressing her jealousy of Warren's philandering and his state of mind? It's interesting to think so. Certainly she was self-aware enough to admit in another collage, "I react like everyone else, even those I most despise, so I make up for it by deploring every action I commit, good or bad."

Not just content with acting, she explored other means of self-expression. At the urging of Buck Henry, Warren's co-director on *Heaven Can Wait*, she made a seventeen-minute documentary about her sister, entitled *What Does Dorrie Want?* It would be shown at the Filmex festival in Los Angeles in early 1982, where it received a very favorable response. What is basically an interview with Diane's closest family member sounds more like an interview with herself: In fits and starts Dorrie admits she wants peace and security and motherhood. Diane also began to explore the possibility of expressing herself through the written word. Having scribbled her thoughts on paper for many years, she began to collaborate seriously on a screenplay of Mary Gordon's novel, *Final Payments*, with Bo

Goldman. They had become close following the tragic death of his twenty-two-year-old son in an automobile accident; Diane reached out to help when many of his friends found it easier not to get involved.

The biggest project Diane would involve herself with in 1982 was not another film but her favorite hobby, photography. With Marvin Heiferman, the Castelli Gallery's director of photography, who she worked with in 1979 on her exhibition and book of photographs, *Reservations*, she began to research the "still" libraries of all the major Hollywood film studios. She had the help of Joe Kelly, a photographer whom she had been friendly with for several years, and who would become increasingly involved with her affairs over the next few years. The result, published in 1983, was the book *Still Life*. Beautifully executed, with superb art direction by Lloyd Ziff, the book humorously points out the reality of Hollywood's celluloid image in studio stills from the 1940s to the 1960s. From Lassie, on the cover, to Ronald Reagan and Jane Wyman "Relaxing at Home" (Ronnie is lying on a chaise longue on a perfectly manicured lawn by a perfectly blue pool, trying to look natural while woodenly sucking in his gut), there's a wonderfully impish sense of humor in the publicity stills, chosen mainly from B-movies.

In her introductory essay, entitled "Appearances Are Deceptive," Diane intelligently discusses the Hollywood star syndrome. The underlying theme reinforces how much entrapment she feels in the goldfish bowl of scrutiny that is the lot of every public figure.

Yet there is a certain longing when she writes, "I remember at the end of movies I liked—movies with happy endings—it thrilled me to think that life was reduced to a fixed, happy moment in time. I was really susceptible to the idea life, in the best possible way, was a dream."

Tellingly, none of the fourteen films Diane had made had a happy ending, and the next two roles she would play, back to back, also did not.

Diane's quest for new horizons took her out of the country on location for nearly a year during 1983. At first glance *The Little Drummer Girl* seemed like a wonderful idea. With talented director George Roy Hill, of *Butch Cassidy and the Sundance Kid* and *The World According to Garp* fame, backed by John le Carré's best-selling novel with a political message about the Palestinians and Israelis fighting for a homeland, as well as a *very* big budget, courtesy of Warner Brothers, it is no wonder that Diane was tempted. Also, in the part, she would get to play classical theater, from Shakespeare to Shaw to Wilde. As it happened, the theatrical scenes of Diane, as Charlie, a rather inadequate actress treading the boards in repertory theater in the English hinterland, are some of the best in the movie. Hill and screenwriter Loring Mandel should have been warned when, after a three-day session in le Carré's chalet in Switzerland, Hill felt, "Great. Now we've got an eight-hour film."

It felt like it. The plot is almost too difficult to describe: Charlie is a pro-PLO actress who gets psychologically blackmailed into working for the Israeli secret service by an agent she's attracted to, who's pretending to be a member of the PLO, and who, as part of her mission, she is meant to be in love with so that the PLO will accept her, so that she can train in a PLO camp to assassinate a respected figure of the Zionist movement, in order that the Israelis can assassinate a major PLO terrorist, so that . . . Charlie didn't know whether she's coming or going, and neither did the audience.

To be fair to Diane, her performance is superb, given the material she had to work with, but in this case even her most supportive critics found it difficult to say anything nice. Even the ever-faithful Vincent Canby was hard put to say anything more positive than, "In particular, Miss Keaton, a fine actress, is left high and dry by the screenplay." Only David Denby in *New York* magazine gave the film a positive review, stating that "Diane Keaton gives a performance of sensitivity and force." It wasn't Diane's fault, although she admits she didn't achieve what she was looking for in the role. "I just didn't pull that one off. I tried very hard, but when I look back on that one, it was just *effort*." Perhaps Richard Schickel in *Time* put it best: "The trouble with John le Carré's 1983 novel, *The Little Drummer Girl*, was that it required more than 400 pages of densely detailed writing to lend credence to an improbable plot that a writer less impressed by his own critical repute might have skipped through in about half the length."

Diane did get to spend five months on location in England, Greece, and West Germany, which might seem like a vacation to some, and which one critic wickedly called "a production manager's dream," though filming on the West Bank of Israeli-occupied territory in 105-degree heat certainly was not. In retrospect, given Charlie's PLO leanings, it's a pity that Diane didn't pass the role on to Vanessa Redgrave, as revenge for up-staging her evening of triumph at the 1977 Academy Awards.

From Europe and the Middle East, Diane traveled west to Canada and Pittsburgh for her next film. While she had been excited by the concept of playing a politically motivated actress who becomes embroiled and finally destroyed by the harsh real-ity of political expediency in *Little Drummer Girl*, the title role in *Mrs. Soffel* was dearer to her heart. First of all she would be working with the talented Australian director of *My Brilliant Career*, Gillian Armstrong, whom she'd wanted to work with for some time. Diane, having struggled for so long to create a sepa-rate identity for herself as a performer is naturally drawn to other women who have achieved the same recognition in the arts. Secondly, the true story of Kate Soffel, the devout and righteous wife of the warden of the Allegheny County Prison, who shocked Victorian America in 1901 by falling in love with a small-time crook, Ed Biddle, who'd been convicted of the murder of a local grocer in a holdup, was too compelling to turn down. While trying to save Biddle's soul before he faced the hangman's noose, Mrs. Soffel fell under his spell, and helped him and his brother, Jack, also convicted, to escape, fleeing to Canada with them.

It's easy to see why the outwardly pure, Bible-toting Kate Soffel, torn between love for her husband and children and wifely duty, yet finally succumbing to a grand passion, would appeal to Diane; Mrs. Soffel was a woman who gave up everything and achieved notoriety for love. Also cast was Edward Herrmann, as the warden husband, Peter Soffel, whom she'd acted with in *Reds*, and the charismatic, American-born, young Australian actor Mel Gibson, who'd come to international prominence in the Australian films, *Road Warrior* and *Gallipoli*.

There was a very strong attraction between Diane and Gibson; rarely has she been so forthright about her attraction to a man as she was about him. "It was tremendously exciting to do that scene in the jail with Mel when he takes the saw out of my boots, and I'm reading something from the Bible and saying, 'I'm nothing,' and he was flirting with me, and I was thinking, 'Well that's the most fun I've ever had' with Mel looking up at me like that."

Another statement about Mel Gibson is even more telling in that she doesn't seem to differentiate between playing the role and real life: "It was great to be in love with him, he's just so great, it's like whaaaaa, my God. See, I thought he was great, I think he's got a real emotional base to him. What's hard about being this woman who falls in love? It's like her life opens up because this guy is just like, ahhhh, it's just magic." Diane sounds more like a teenager in love for the first time than a mature woman in her late thirties. It is interesting to wonder what would have happened after they'd finished the film if Gibson hadn't been married. Given Diane's admitted attraction to actors, it sounds as if true romance transcended the plot.

This wasn't an easy location shoot either. In the final escape and chase scenes they worked under intolerable conditions, with a wind chill factor of minus twenty degrees. One has to think of the problems of filming in snow: You can't have footprints from previous takes messing up pristine white surface in what's supposed to be the wilderness, so after every take crews have to go out and fill in the footprints, and then sweep over the surface till it looks virgin again. Director Armstrong said of the experience, "You find yourself screaming a lot. Thank God I was working with real troupers. Had anyone been the least bit temperamental, it'd have been a nightmare."

The effort paid off, and Gillian Armstrong's first American film was lauded by the critics, who praised not only her direction, but also Ron Nyswaner's script and the performances, including those of Herrmann and Matthew Modine, who played Jack Biddle. Keaton and Gibson were obviously singled out, and it looked as though Metro Goldwyn Mayer's gamble in rushing the film through for release in the final week for Academy Award consideration (the seven days before January 1) would pay off. It didn't, but at least Diane was back on track after the disaster of *The Little Drummer Girl*, which had been released only two months before.

Diane's location work had of course finished much earlier in the summer, and she was back home at last. It was a cathartic period for her, although she said later, "I don't want to do that ever again . . . I felt like I'd left my life for quite some time. I felt alone." But it was probably what she needed at the time.

Waiting for her in New York was the huge, stark penthouse on Central Park West that she had bought when she was with Beatty, and the only company she would have now would be her beloved cats. The surreal, time-warped atmosphere of a location shoot, when one gets so close to the actors and crew was over. Now she had to return to the reality of life alone and decide what to do next, which isn't necessarily easy for an actress as famous as Diane Keaton.

10

FAME AND FORTUNE

Diane's apartment, high above Central Park West, has windows on all four sides, and is painted white on white on white—everything is white, including the furniture and the dinner service. Everything is also terribly neat; there is absolutely no clutter anywhere, but somehow the Keaton personality comes through. In the foyer there is a sculpture, which on close inspection turns out to be hundreds of artificial yellow bananas arranged by Keaton, and inside the apartment are huge flower arrangements, and curios picked out by Keaton on her travels—a plastic bust of Pope John Paul II, and a trio of reindeer she found in Massachusetts.

The location and the view—Central Park, with Woody's Fifth Avenue penthouse across the way, the towers of midtown Manhattan to the south, the Hudson River to the west, and, to the north, Harlem and the Bronx—so removed from the antlike figures of ordinary people going about their business in the streets below, indicates that this snug aerie is the home of someone very powerful, rich, and famous. Yet the interior is so simple, without the usual trappings of wealth that one normally finds in apartments such as this, that one wonders about the person who lives here. An indication is given in the art, which is constantly changing, but most likely to include one of Diane's collages and some of her photographs. This is the home of a creative person, whose house is a private sanctuary, who is unconcerned with making an impression. Even the Oscar is nowhere to be seen. Part of the idiosyncrasy of this apartment is that although it has a huge white gleaming kitchen and a large dining room, it isn't a showcase backdrop for lavish entertaining.

An earlier remark, to writer Penelope Gilliatt in *The New Yorker* about her old apartment on East 68th Street, equally describes the new. "My apartment isn't really finger-marked enough to be convincing, you know? It's my own fault that I haven't anyone to cook for. Of course I'm a lousy cook. But it is a fault. I'd have to order those things you're always supposed to have by you. I can't seem to need them. Flour, milk, tea, tomatoes, bacon, bread, coffee, onions. I buy them all the time, but they're always going bad." Even now, when she could afford it, Diane doesn't have a cook or any servants; basically, the apartment serves as a refuge for Diane and her cats. Certainly it does not seem like the home of a major movie star.

But that is exactly what Diane Keaton is in the 1980s. She can have any part she wants, and name her own price, but, still, deep down inside she doesn't quite realize who she is in the eyes of the public. Yes, she only has to pick up a paper or a magazine to see herself mentioned yet again, but it's almost as though it wasn't her—that's *Diane Keaton*, not the naïve Diane Hall who still sees herself as a basic California girl. Of course, she's come a long way since she arrived in New York, accompanied by her parents, fifteen years before. But inside, like all of us, she sees herself as the same person she was as a child. Even the tardy education she received, from her exposure to people like Woody, which has turned her into a widely read and highly intelligent woman, hasn't really affected her perception of herself as someone who never believes she's good enough.

Obviously she has come to terms with her life and status,

how could she not with the media sniffing out her every last movement, especially through two very publicized affairs with two of the most famous men in the country, and all those flashbulbs popping off in front of her dark glasses. But Diane accepts this side of what acting has done with reluctance—to her it has nothing to do with her craft. This is no act; she is simply very shy. She would far rather go about the normal, if trying, everyday business of living in New York, than be the target of publicity at some premiere or another.

Her wish to be a part of the city, like every New Yorker, walking on the streets, popping into shops, discovering new things, and, in her case, going to classes and taking photographs is not an affectation; it's simply how she is. She sees herself as a normal person and all she asks is to be left alone. While many might find this hard to believe, it's a genuine reaction to her fame. And it is also true that Diane does not equate all the publicity surrounding Diane Keaton to herself. Even now she can't quite believe the power of her name. In 1985, when Dominick Dunne interviewed her for *Vanity Fair*, he recalls asking her if he could drop her name to get a table at the chic Venice restaurant, 72 Market Street, owned by Dudley Moore among others, which is always booked up for days. Diane's reaction was, "It won't help."

"Yes, it will," replied Dunne.

Of course it did!

Without a doubt, most of us would love to be famous. That's why we buy all those magazines about our favorite stars, constantly intrigued by the gossip about every personality, whatever their walk of life. Even the garish covers of the tabloids we see in the lines at the supermarket, while patently untrue, fascinate us—but for the most part the desire to be famous is psychologically only a desire to be loved. For someone who has gone through that, like Diane, the most important thing is to be *really* loved, on a personal level. The trappings of fame are not the end result, they are a byproduct of what she wants to do in life, which is acting, or being involved in film in other ways.

While stardom is wonderful in its own way, it is not the be all and end all. As Diane put it so well in 1977 when she won the Oscar, "It's been a strange and wonderful year, but I feel slightly removed from it all. I've always thought of acting as an art to be practiced. But I'd be a fool to say the idea of receiving attention isn't kind of interesting. When you're doing it, that's what matters. Getting there, and being famous, are the hard parts."

Diane's friends agree that her preference for anonymity is without guile. "She disavows all the trappings of fame," says writer Lynn Grossman. Her dear friend, Kathryn Grody, agrees, "She's not waiting in line for heads to turn at the Russian Tea Room." Diane will stand in line at a movie house, and has been known to decline offers by theater managers to pass her in ahead of the crowd. Says Dunne in his *Vanity Fair* article, which captured her so well, "She's almost too good to be true, for a movie star."

One of the reasons Diane is wary of fame is because she finds it makes her too introspective. Once she said, rather philosophically, "Being known has its problems. It's a little bit harder to grow up and have a sense of humor about your life. Because you have a lot of attention, you have a tendency to put yourself under a microscope. I don't think other people care, but *you* tend to think about yourself too much."

And while Diane is naturally introspective, she doesn't like to dwell on herself too much. It brings out all her insecurities and her inclination to put herself down. Her fear of fame is that she doesn't feel she deserves it. "I think I like to deny it. It suits me to deny it, but I suppose that's another one of my problems.

"Look, I don't think it's such a big deal. I don't think I'm that big a thing . . . You see, I'm not an idol or anything like that." To her, being famous is like being Woody or Warren or Jack Nicholson, who she sees as being instantly recognizable on the street. Her much discussed personal style, which has evolved into almost an art form of layer upon layer of different shapes, silhouettes, and colors, is possibly a manifestation of her insecurity. Contrarily, it works as a disguise, and Diane is quite right when people don't recognize her on the streets. They certainly turn around and take notice of this chic, if somewhat eccentric figure, who can be seen shopping on Columbus Avenue, or checking out the galleries on 57th Street, or finding new curios in SoHo.

It's also fair to say that Diane's search for anonymity is a defense mechanism, especially with regard to her private life. Why she has been accused of being inarticulate so often is that she finds it easier to appear dumb than answer questions she considers embarrassing. Her love affairs with Woody and Warren, which definitely propelled her into the public eye as much as her acting, are also possibly a source of pain to her. She is, first and foremost, a sensitive, romantic woman. That these affairs and other loves never worked out for her cannot be easy. She is so secretive about her love life that even her father, Jack, says, "Even *I* don't ask her what's going on." After she got over Warren she started to date the director of *Reckless*, James Foley, but this relationship didn't work out either.

It's significant that she is strong enough to keep on being friends with her ex-lovers. She still talks to Woody nearly every day, and has become great friends with Mia Farrow, Woody's current love and the mother of his child. While no doubt she must sometimes wonder, "What if that were I?", any sadness or regret she might have at the lost opportunity of not being the mother of his child herself is buried under her love and friendship for Woody and Mia. That their relationship has endured so long and through all the changes that have occurred to Diane and Woody is a testament to the depth of their admiration for each other.

Yet on the other hand they don't seem to be so different from Alvy and Annie either. Recently Diane, Woody, and Mia were having dinner at Elaine's, the famous Italian restaurant on the Upper East Side of New York that Woody frequents, and as the three of them were leaving Diane went straight to Woody's waiting limo. Woody called after her, "Diane, that's not the right car." Diane paid no attention and got inside. Eventually Woody realized that it was his car, got in with Mia, and said, "I can't believe I don't know my own car." As the limo was drawing away a waiter came running out of the restaurant with Diane's wallet, appointment book, and other odds and ends that she had left behind. Talk about life imitating art, it's too like an Allen comedy to be true.

Diane has also remained friends with Warren. Despite the obvious hurt she suffered after they broke up, when she wouldn't allow anyone to mention his name, they too have remained very close. Beatty has, naturally, been associated with many women since he and Diane parted ways, including Mary Tyler Moore—who lives in the other Art Deco tower of Diane's building on Central Park West, and who Diane could see through her windows if she so desired—Jessica Savitch, the newscaster who was tragically killed in a car accident, Isabel Adjani, the beautiful French film actress, and a whole bevy of beautiful models. Yet he and Diane have remained so close that when the Toronto Film Festival paid tribute to Warren Beatty on September 10, 1984, Diane was in the audience. Admittedly, when Warren paid tribute to her acting and influence on him, she would not stand to be acknowledged, but she was there. That they are in constant communication with each other is illustrated by a story told by Dominick Dunne in *Vanity Fair*. The day after their last talk, Dunne was in the Polo Lounge of the Beverly Hills Hotel, and Beatty came by, stopped at the table, and said, "I hear you had an interesting day yesterday." He was meeting Diane for lunch, in itself unusual, as Diane normally avoids such high-profile places in L.A., preferring to stay at the Shangri-La Hotel in Santa Monica, which has become a favorite among the more discreet movie crowd. The hotel is also a little different, being a renovated nineteen-forties' apartment hotel. But then, as Kathryn Grody says, "Diane likes the funkier kind of places."

While Diane may put herself down and worry about her life, her loves, and her talent, she is honest enough to admit that she does have an ego. "Let's just say that straight out. I definitely do. About work? I don't know. What can I say about it? I'm not going to say I liked my work. Forget it. I did the work, you comment on it. It's out there. It's over. It's finished. It's history."

And while she may dismiss her past performances, she is astute enough to want to control her future work. She is well aware of her power in the Hollywood scene and her ability to command high fees depends on the success of her films. As the adage goes, "You're only as good as your last movie."

As far back as 1981, Diane, like Barbra Streisand, Goldie Hawn, and other powerful Hollywood actresses, found that the best way for her to find the right vehicle for herself was to produce it. In February 1982 it was announced that she would coproduce *Modern Bride*, a comedy about a woman of a certain age who gets married for the first time as her parents get a divorce. Everything was set: Richard Roth, whose last film had been *Julia* would co-produce, and MGM/UA would provide financing. Unfortunately it never got made, and Diane went on to make *Crimes of the Heart* with Freddie Fields who had backed the idea. Such is the convoluted history of Hollywood.

To the average person, the months and years between films sound as though actors have an easy life. To a certain extent that's true, but the preparation for a film can take a year, with all the major participants, especially the director and producer, working full time with the writers to achieve a working script and looking for financing. But this doesn't mean that Diane was constantly involved with her film projects; she was sometimes left with time to enjoy a favorite pastime.

Diane loves to drive across the country, and part of that enjoyment is because she can behave like any other tourist. Road travel also appeals to her tastes for the simple. For instance, she loves McDonald's McBLTs. You can't see Diane running into the McDonald's on the Upper West Side without drawing attention to herself and making all the gossip columns the next day. But away from the city lights she can. Her friend Lynn

Grossman, who travels with her quite frequently, describes this down-to-earth Diane as someone who likes hanging out and stopping for fries at a roadside stand, and singing songs along the way.

Diane's trips also appeal to something in her aesthetic sensibility that's drawn to tackiness. As with her collection of kitsch religious mementos, she enjoys experiencing the more plastic side of American culture, staying in cheap motels and once taking a trip with Grossman to Graceland, the Elvis shrine in Memphis. Drawn as she is to the tasteless theater of something like Graceland, she is just as attracted to the purity of the southwestern desert in Arizona and New Mexico. Kathryn Grody, who also travels with her often, says, "She likes any odd, out-of-the-way, eccentric nook or cranny, like the diner most people wouldn't even stop at."

It was on one of these trips that Diane found the inspiration for a project that was to occupy her for three years and become her most personal film statement.

11

HEAVEN

Diane first conceived the idea of making a documentary film about heaven back in the summer of 1982 on one of her car trips across America. Traveling with her friend Kristi Zea, who had been the production designer for *Interiors* and *Shoot the Moon*, they stopped by the Visitors Center of the Mormon Temple in Salt Lake City. Part of the conducted tour was a promotional film about what the "lucky few" could expect to see when they reaped their just rewards and achieved heaven! Diane was fascinated by the concept of interpreting and depicting heaven—especially at this point in her life when she was in search of her own identity and worth. She started wondering how other religions and individuals conceived of the notion of a hereafter, and, with her visually oriented mind, of how many different ways heaven had been depicted in works of art and in the cinema.

The concept of *Heaven* became a passion for her, and soon she was researching every bit of material she could find on the subject. Avidly she searched out every vision of the notion and began to collect film footage, tapes of old television shows, books, and religious icons. It was almost as though she was on an epic shopping spree for the eternal, and like her passion for searching out old clothes and knickknacks as presents for friends, it became a central part of her life.

Buoyed by the success of her short documentary, *What Does Dorrie Want?*, at the Filmex Festival in Los Angeles, Diane decided to make a documentary about heaven. She asked her friend, Joe Kelly (who, since collaborating with her on *Still Life*, was working as an editor at Ariel Books), if he would consider producing the film for her. He was enthusiastic about the project, as were her friends Kathryn Grody and Carol Kane, and one has to assume that Woody and Warren also supported the project. Diane and Joe formed a company, aptly named Perpetual Productions, Inc., to produce it. Yet as Diane and Kelly envisioned the film, a montage of film clips and interviews with people relating their personal concept of heaven, it was obviously difficult to sell. *Heaven* certainly didn't seem to be anything that would appeal at the box office, but eventually Tom Kuhn and Charles Mitchell, who had just formed RVP Productions (formerly RCA Video Productions) became interested. She was introduced to them by her manager Arlyne Rothberg, who became executive producer of the film. RCA agreed to finance the documentary and show it as a sixty-minute film on their new cable-TV network.

Much in the same way Warren started with *Reds*, Diane and Joe started to interview everyone they knew who had a strong feeling about an afterlife, taping the interviews on video equipment in her Central Park West apartment, with Kelly as the cinematographer. Everyone was roped into the project, from friends to her housekeeper and the doorman of her building. Their questions were very general: "What kind of place do you think heaven is?" "What does heaven look like?" "What kind of rewards do you think heaven holds?" and so on. These early interviews, conducted in November 1984, made Diane realize that people had very strong views about heaven.

When the money was assured, Diane and Joe started in earnest, ordering films from religious catalogues, and starting to comb film archives from the Museum of Modern Art in New York and the Hollywood studios. They were helped in this task by the film historian William K. Everson, and it was on his advice that Diane researched clips from German film studios when she was in Munich for *The Little Drummer Girl*. (*Heaven* would take nearly three years to come to the screen as Diane had to interrupt production three times while she shot *Drummer Girl*, *Mrs. Soffel*, and *Crimes of the Heart*.)

Diane loved the whole process of looking at movies for references to heaven. "My appetite for old footage just grew into a monster," and, according to Joe, managed to exasperate "at least three assistant editors in the process." She's always loved watching films, as she told Joan Juliet Buck in *Vanity Fair*. "Maybe what I'll do in heaven is look at images forever and select them. I have amassed a huge library of images—kissing scenes from movies, pictures I like. Visual things are really key for me. As a kid I used to love looking at pictures, magazines, catalogues—everything." It was such an enjoyable job that eventually they had to install a computer to log in all the hours of footage she amassed. The material was broken down into categories such as "Eyes," "Roses," "Death," and "Mystic Visions" and ranged from such classic films as *Metropolis* and *Beauty and the Beast*, to a rather distasteful vision of a racially segregated heaven in the 1936 film, *Green Pastures*. Diane says the footage from *The Horn Blows at Midnight* made her "start thinking heaven was more frightening than hell." Unfortunately, many of the clips Diane wanted for the documentary were not available, either because they were too expensive or because people wouldn't release the rights. MGM—Diane had just worked for them on *Mrs. Soffel*—was an exception; they allowed her to use clips from their archives for free, charging her only for the print costs.

Eventually Joe Kelly prevailed on Diane that the film had to have a balance, and they started to concentrate on filming the interviews in February 1985. Most of them were conducted in

Los Angeles. For many reasons Diane perceived her native city as the perfect backdrop for the interviews. There are more religious cults there, and, as she says, "I felt California is the place where people come frequently, dreamers . . . It's like Nathanael West, and things like that." Much in the same way Diane perceived the artificiality of the situations in which actors were photographed for the publicity stills she'd used in *Still Life*, making them "truly indefinable" and therefore immortal, so she felt the fakeness of Hollywood would be the richest source of interview material. It's obtuse logic, but that's how Diane's mind works!

Barbara Ling, who'd worked with Diane on the short about Dorrie, was called in as art director, and between her, Diane, Joe, and cinematographer Frederick Elmes they conceived of the stylized approach of photographing the subjects. Geometrically shaped highlights of different colored light were projected across their faces, set against angular surreal sets they'd constructed in a studio in Venice, California.

Carol Kane joined Diane and Joe in their search for the offbeat people Diane wanted in the film. Some, like an old woman, Grace, who they spotted scurrying across Hollywood Boulevard to the Tick-Tock Studio, were difficult to persuade to consent to the filming. Diane worked for months on Grace until she finally gave in and said yes to Diane's winning smile.

The range of interviews was considerable, from "ordinary" people like Grace, to minor celebrities like Peter Sellers's youngest daughter, Victoria, accompanied by Kenny Ostin, the son of the head of Warner Brothers Records, who Diane and Joe picked up on Rodeo Drive, to the Reverend Hands, an Old Testament–style preacher working with drunks at the Last Chance Mission in Venice, to the boxing promoter Don King, who asked in return that Diane watch a prize fight in Las Vegas, where at ringside she was sandwiched between Muhammed Ali and Larry Holmes. One of the most terrifying anticipated interviews for Diane was with the fire-breathing evangelist Dr. Hymers, but when she met him after one of his doom-laden sermons he turned out to be a total fan. Of course, this didn't stop him from trying to convert her in a Hollywood restaurant!

Heaven tells as much about Keaton as it does about people's beliefs and images. The hesitant style to the interviews, conducted by Diane offscreen, is much like her own manner of speech. It's obvious from the film that everyone she corralled into being interviewed, including her own family members, is searching for the truth of their vision of heaven. Diane understood this, as she takes the time to make statements that are as thought out as possible, delaying for time by the trick of utilizing expletives and stuttering.

Heaven became such a big project that RVP Productions provided additional financing to turn it into a full-length documentary of eighty minutes for theatrical release, to be distributed by Island Pictures. Cutting all the footage took eighteen months, and at the end of production Diane presented all the editors with watches inscribed with a line from the film, "A year seems like five minutes." The focus and viewpoint of the film changed during this process; fifteen minutes of images about death were cut, as were many of the interviews, including one with the Christian Motorcycle Club in Garden Grove, which sounds as though it would have been hilarious.

Diane was surprised that when it came time to show the finished film it was harder to do than watch herself in one of her own films. "It's very hard to separate yourself," she said. "Watching your film with an audience is harder than anything, even harder than watching yourself. It's the panic of all panics." Remember, this came from the actress who had never seen any of her early films, from *Lovers and Other Strangers* to *Annie Hall*. At the first public screening Diane had to get up and leave.

So emotionally involved with the film was Diane that it must have been heartrending for her to read the reviews when the film came out in April 1987. To say the critics were not thrilled by it is an understatement. The rather curious way the film was structured was not to its advantage. Perhaps Marliane Glicksman in *Film Comment* said it best: "*Heaven* is constructed the way Keaton appears to think: a burst of thought, followed by another, a doubling back and then forward, bundles of thoughts propelled by emotion (rather than vice versa), thoughts that vary in cadence and emotions that vary in intensity. Her thoughts are conceptual, her thinking creative, associative rather than linear."

Some of the critics preferred the film clips to the interviews, although Canby in *The New York Times* called the former "a lot of defenseless Hollywood junk." Canby, who has always strongly supported Diane, felt the film was so bad that he questioned every aspect of it, from suggesting that the set was something more appropriate to a *Vogue* magazine fashion shoot to the whole premise of the film, calling it "dumbfoundingly silly" and a "conceit imposed on its subjects." That Canby found the film patronizing must have been very hard for Diane, but then, she'd had the guts to go out and make a personal statement, and that was most important to her.

Undoubtedly she made mistakes with *Heaven*, probably the greatest being not to identify the interviewees—just as Warren had not in *Reds*. Even her family members weren't identified, which was all the more poignant as the interview with her grandmother, Mary, made famous and immortalized as Grammy Hall by Woody in *Annie Hall*, was one of the last times Diane saw her alive. She died just after the interview, aged ninety-four, still not believing in heaven, even though she was a Catholic. Diane's respect for Mary Hall is manifest when she says, "She was one of the few people who had the courage to say that she doesn't think there is going to be anything, and I thought this particularly amazing when you get so close to the point where you're going to say goodbye to life." The death of this wonderful woman, who'd been so supportive of Diane from the very start of her acting career, was the end of a very long chapter in Diane's life.

Diane had not only learned from Grammy Hall, but also from the experience of making *Heaven*. Stubborn as her grandmother, she was now, more than ever, anxious to continue to produce and direct films. She had finally found, if not her idea of heaven, at least a métier that satisfied her need for creativity in this world.

12

LIFE AFTER *HEAVEN*

In the introduction to her book, *Still Life*, Diane Keaton said, "I was really susceptible to the idea that life, in the best possible way, was a dream. Happiness was something that you wanted to grab on to and stop. Heaven seemed a notion where everything was perfect; and by being perfect, heaven was motionless."

There is obviously a fear in Diane Keaton of stagnating. She can't stand keeping still. She has to have something to occupy herself with all the time. It could be that she's simply looking for new challenges for herself. But most of all, she's a fighter determined to succeed and extend her range.

Even before *Heaven* was completed, Diane went back to acting for the silver screen, after a hiatus of over a year and a half. She herself had optioned the project when Beth Henley's Pulitzer Prize–winning play, *Crimes of the Heart*, was first staged at the Manhattan Theatre Club in 1980 (it subsequently moved to Broadway). Diane was intrigued by the dramatic possibilities of this story of three diametrically different sisters reunited by the incident of the youngest shooting her politician husband in the stomach, because she "didn't like his stinking looks!"

Diane had seen it as a marvelous comedy vehicle for herself and got Henley to co-write the screenplay with Jonathan Demme, who would direct. It was a difficult project not only to cast but also to finance; eventually Freddie Fields, who had produced *Goodbar* and was then head of production at MGM, agreed to produce *Crimes* in 1983. He brought in the brilliant young Australian director, Bruce Beresford, who had made a name for himself with *Breaker Morant* and *Tender Mercies*, and managed to get Sissy Spacek and Jessica Lange to commit to the other two leads. Everything seemed set, and Hollywood cynics gleefully predicted that the set, with these three highly individualistic Academy Award–winning actresses on it, would be a cat fight. But the demise of Beresford's standing in movietown, due to his disastrous 1985 film, *King David*, in which Richard Gere makes a fool of himself in an unendurable retelling of the biblical tale of King David making a fool of himself over Bathsheba, caused financing to dry up. Fields now needed to find eight or nine million dollars to get the production underway—the three ladies were taking a seventy-five percent cut in their normal fees—and eventually obtained it from the flamboyant Italian producer, Dino de Laurentiis.

Interestingly, until just before shooting commenced on May 5, 1986, it had never been decided which of the three sisters would be played by which of the three Oscar-winning women. Finally it was settled that Diane would play Lenny MaGrath, a spinster who had never left the family home in Hazlehurst, Mississippi, and yearns for love but is afraid that men won't like her because of an "underdeveloped ovary." Jessica Lange would play the middle sister, Meg, a bourbon-soaked, man-hungry singer who has failed in Los Angeles and has come home from trying to "dry out." The role of the irrepressible youngest sister, Babe MaGrath Botrelle, under arrest for the attempted murder of her husband, who she shoots when he discovers her in the back of a car with a fifteen-year-old black boy, would be for Spacek.

Diane had always thought that Lenny was the best role for

her, admitting, "I guess I never thought I was flamboyant enough for Babe." For a long while, even though she'd been the catalyst for the project, she wasn't sure she could play the part, partially because of the accent, and partially because she had become somewhat ambivalent about acting again. "I have such mixed feelings about acting," she told Joan Juliet Buck. "You go through so many phases. There was a time when I was really concerned about what I did. The buzz that happened with *Annie Hall* was extremely exciting and extremely terrifying. . . . It's a different time for me. I will never be that famous again. Those days are gone, and it's different as you get older. . . . The fun is when it *goes,* when the acting is alive."

Her problems with the accent were alleviated by several months of training with dialogue coach Nora Dunfee (who had coached Mel Gibson with his American accent for *Mrs. Soffel*) to get the Southern drawl down pat. Coaching from Marilyn Fried, who Diane still uses for every film she does, soon washed away her insecurities about her acting not being alive anymore, and the interaction between the three stars made this one of her happiest films.

Fears of the three not getting along, which even Fields admitted to having, proved unfounded. As Lange put it, "No one has any desperate need to be center stage. We've all been there," and they got on better than anyone had predicted, even eschewing the regulation trailers for a house with the three bedrooms turned into dressing rooms and a shared kitchen, living room, and swimming pool, that began to resemble a cross between a girls dormitory and a day-care center, with Spacek's four-year-old daughter, Schuyler, and Lange's four-year-old daughter, Shura (by Mikhail Baryshnikov), and infant Hannah, by Sam Shepard. And if that wasn't complicated enough, playwright Shepard was acting in the film as Doc Peters, an old beau of Meg's, who Lenny secretly yearned for!

The comic interaction between the three impossible, diverse sisters in *Crimes* was an interesting contrast not only of performance, but also of technique. Margy Rochlin, writing for

American Film, described their ways of preparing for a scene: "On one side, Spacek is grimacing slightly and mouthing to herself. Lange is flapping her arms vigorously and gulping huge, deep breaths of air. Meanwhile, Keaton, with eyes closed, is hip-hopping around the room accompanied by the tinny squeal of her Walkman at full throttle." (Diane was more than likely listening to Julio Iglesias, whose music she apparently adores.)

It was a difficult role for her to play. She had to get the right feeling of an embittered woman who feels that life, and men, have passed her by, while retaining the intrinsic comedy of Henley's Lenny. It couldn't have been easy for her, at forty, to pat her chin when one of the sisters remarks, "We're all getting old," while blowing out the candles on her birthday cookies. Yet perhaps more of Diane was in Lenny than she realized. Actors, more than most people realize, wear something of their own in films for the special significance it has for them. One of the most noticeable pieces of the dowdy ill-fitting clothes Diane wore as Lenny was a big sloppy sweater in a nondescript shade of green, which had once belonged to Kathryn Grody's mother. The only adornment she wore in the film was a cameo brooch, bequeathed to her by Mary Hall. But perhaps the most significant part of her wardrobe was the same tall crowned, floppy brimmed hat that first made her such a fashion figure in *Annie Hall*, then saw her through the rigors of *Reds*. In *Crimes* one can almost sense that she used it as her way of identifying with Lenny, a reminder of the two great loves that had passed her by. There was a lot about the role that she could identify with, including having two younger sisters of her own. "I have two sisters, and that kind of psychological makeup—the kind of rivalries and love and envy, in particular Lenny's envy of Meg—is fascinating to me."

Although there is a pathos to Lenny, the role was also comic, and Diane found the location an easy one. Her general sense of humor and exuberant spirits were very much in evidence off the set. The three women had all taken houses on the beach for the duration of the filming and these were the scenes for easy "family" get-togethers that included Shepard and Lange; Spacek with her husband, scenic designer (now director) Jack Fisk, and Beresford and his longtime companion, journalist Virginia Duigan, who gave birth to their baby, Trilby, during the middle of filming. Diane's beach house was obviously less crowded, though she had her family and close friends like Carol Kane stay with her.

Beresford remembers one weekend, when they all came over to his house, and Diane, who's passionate about Trivial Pursuit, organized a game that went on all day, with the men and the women playing against each other. "It was me, Sam Shepard, Jack Fisk, and David Carpenter [who plays a young lawyer in the film]. The women won. We didn't have a chance, they were so bloody good."

The extent of the rapport that the three actresses achieved was witnessed by journalist Joan Goodman, of *USA Today*, on the last day of filming. They were so comfortable with each other and knew each other so well that they were able to kid around as only old friends can. Diane asked Lange where the wrap party would be, and Lange, straight-faced, said, "It's at your house, and you're going to cook." This caused some laughter, given Diane's well-known lack of culinary skills, and then both Lange and Diane started to tease Spacek, who had a virus and whose voice had lowered an octave, with "You're beginning to sound like Debra Winger." A little later the three of them were avidly pouring over the latest copy of *People* magazine, which none of them like to appear in too often. "I hate to be the subject of gossip," says Lange. "I just like to read it."

"Oh, yeah," responded Diane sarcastically. "Really? Well, I am surprised." This caused all three of them to break up!

The filming of *Crimes* was a new experience for Diane in many ways. Not only was it a comeback to comedy, her first in nearly ten years, but the interaction with two other leading ladies was completely different from anything she'd done before, even *Interiors*. She was also on a far more open set than ever before. Southport, North Carolina, with its easygoing ways, and the involvement of the townspeople, was something she had not previously experienced to such a degree. Apart from very close friends and people she trusts, Diane tends to remain alone when she is in the middle of a role. The irrepressible Southerns couldn't quite understand that. On one occasion she was sitting in a restaurant and a man asked her to dance. Diane politely declined his invitation, to which he responded, "Why? I don't have any holes in my socks." Then he went on to prove it by taking his shoes off! For once she had no idea how to react.

Besides making *Crimes of the Heart*, 1986 was a very busy year for Diane. She had *Heaven* to finish; she acted in two more films; and she increased her behind-the-camera experience by directing the music video of the rather aptly titled Belinda Carlisle song, "Heaven Is a Place on Earth." She also inspired and curated an exhibition of surreal religious paintings by artist Brent Richardson, which was mounted at the Daniel Wolf Gallery in New York that spring.

The other side of the camera seems to intrigue her more and more as the years go by. Even while she was in the middle of making *Heaven* she and Joe Kelly were working on at least a couple of other film projects. One that seemed all set to go was *The Lemon Sisters*, about three crazy singers in Atlantic City who buy out a nightclub; "All about friendship," says Diane. It would star her two closest friends, Kathryn Grody and Carol Kane, and Diane would not only play the third member of the troupe, but also direct the film. *The Lemon Sisters* didn't get off the ground then, that would happen two years later, although not with Diane directing, only producing.

However, in 1986 Diane did get to sing in a film. It was her long-awaited return to working with Woody, but not the musical he'd been promising to write for her one day, or the comedy he'd promised for Mia Farrow, Diane, and himself. *Radio Days* wasn't written for any of them, although Mia Farrow has one of the biggest roles, as the nightclub singer who becomes a celebrity on the airwaves of fifty years ago. Woody is never seen at all, only his voice is heard describing a boy growing up in a middle-class Jewish family in Rockaway, Queens. One has to wait until the very end of the film to see Diane. She has a cameo role as a nightclub singer. She looks beautiful in a stunning white dress and sounds wonderful singing, "You'd Be So Nice To Come Home To." It wasn't much of an appearance for Diane, "I sang it and left. It was nothing, just half a day. I came in, sang it three times, and I was out." She enjoyed working with Woody, but it wasn't the same as starring in a film with him.

Crimes of the Heart came out in December 1986, to not such good reviews, and *Radio Days* was released shortly later, in February 1987, to extremely good reviews. Diane's nightclub singer was really too small a part for her to get much notice from the critics, but the public loved her. *Crimes* was a different matter; nearly everyone found the film too heavy-handed and all three performances from the stars lacking, though many, like Canby in the *New York Times* and Richard Corliss in *Time*, felt it wasn't their fault. Ironically, one of the best reviews came from the magazine the three actresses are averse to appearing in, *People*. Peter Travers said that it was Diane's strongest work in years. Diane's work was also praised by Kathleen Carroll in the *New York Daily News*, who called her a "jittery comic delight." *Newsweek* also admired her, saying, "Keaton, taking daring chances, takes nervous ticks to delicious, sneaky new highs."

The good reviews must have lessened the blow of the relative failure of Diane's return to comedy, but by the time they came out she was already up to her eyes in diapers, in what the media considered her first comedy since *Annie Hall*. In one sense *Baby Boom* could be called that, as it was the first *light* comedy she'd done since *Annie Hall*, having, as it does, elements of farce and slapstick. Although a topical subject—the working mother—*Baby Boom* is actually more akin to the sophisticated comedies of the forties than the general fare from Hollywood today. For the most part this is due to the style of co-writers Charles Shyer and Nancy Meyers, who had been responsible for another wonderful woman's comedy, *Private Benjamin*.

There was also the style Diane gave the film, in her head-tofoot designer outfits. Working closely with costume designer Susan Becker, the Armani, Cerruti, Karan, Kamali, and Krizia-clad Diane looks like a knockout. Apparently, on the first day of shooting, when Diane walked onto the set the whole crew stopped and stared. Used to her highly individual rummage-sale look they couldn't believe this sophisticated, glamorous lady with a *body* was the layered, hidden Diane everyone knows. Someone, in total admiration, said to her, "You look like . . ." "A female of the species?" laughed Diane.

Even her father approved. Jack, who Diane had given acting lessons to as a birthday present that summer, and Dorothy were employed as extras during the final photography in Los Angeles. He said to Diane, "That's very nice. You have legs." Although Diane made such a fashion statement in *Baby Boom*, and was seen on more covers of more magazines in 1987 than she was in 1977 as Annie Hall, it was just another role for her. She dismissed this new sensual, seductive look for herself, saying "I might keep a couple of things from the film," about the designer finery. (Though, in fact, she has many designer clothes herself; it's just the highly individual way she puts them together that makes them different. For one thing she never wears high heels and never carries a bag, which can change the whole way a woman carries herself.)

It's interesting to ponder that the "new" Diane of the late eighties was the same woman who became such an icon of the seventies in *Annie Hall* and, ten years before that, the ultimate expression of the sixties in *Hair*. It's an indication not only of the stretch of her career, but of how much she is identified with American culture over these two decades. Diane of course disparages it, laughingly saying about her personal style, "Once a hippie, always a hippie."

Baby Boom was a film Diane needed to do. Her last three films had not done well at the box office, and *Crimes* wasn't going to be a wide draw, even though Diane believed in it herself. She needed a vehicle to demonstrate her unique talent for comedy that would be popular with the public, and *Baby Boom* seemed

to be exactly that. It's very difficult for an actress in her powerful position, able to choose anything she wants as a bona fide
"bankable" star to know what to do next. While she was undoubtedly right in choosing projects like *Shoot the Moon* and *Mrs.
Soffel*, which gave us two of the greatest screen performances of
this decade, the films didn't have mass appeal. Diane needed a
popular comedy, and *Baby Boom* was exactly right for her with
its intelligence and sophistication. She couldn't go back to playing a ditzy lady, a problem the talented Goldie Hawn is also
trying to overcome.

When Diane read the script of *Baby Boom*, she realized that
this was the comedy she had been looking for for so long. After
the failure of *Modern Bride* she realized that the film that would
mark her popular comedy comeback needed more substance
than a marriage as a subject, and she jumped at the opportunity
to do it. The concept of a successful, career-oriented woman of
a certain age, faced with unwanted and instant motherhood, appealed to her on many levels, and she instinctively knew it
would have wide audience appeal.

J.C. Wiatt is the quintessential high-powered career woman,
an ultimate Yuppie who's married to her job and living with an
investment banker who's married to his job. At the beginning of
the film, on the way to the most important business meeting of
her life, J.C. finds she's inherited a thirteen-month-old baby
girl, who to her horror—"I went to Yale and Harvard. I . . .
don't have children"—is given to her there and then. J.C. ar-
rives at the Café Pierre for her appointment and, not knowing
what to do with the baby, tries to deposit her at the coat check.
Needless to say, the checker won't accept a baby, and the lun-
cheon meeting is a disaster, losing J.C. the chance to become a
partner in her firm.

The subsequent scenes with J.C. trying to learn how to be a
mother have some wonderful moments, especially the now-
famous one where she tries to give the baby pasta and Perrier
for dinner, not understanding why the baby throws this
gourmet meal all over her, and the room. This sort of behavior

doesn't appeal to her lover, who leaves her for a more secure co-op where he can live with his Eames chairs and Hockney paintings without distraction. J.C., in her turn, decides she can't manage a baby and a career, and leaves New York for Vermont. Her longstanding dream of sometime retiring to the country, now forced upon her earlier than she had planned, turns out to be boring in the extreme. To occupy her time she starts to make apple sauce baby food from her orchard. It's an instant success, and she starts the first gourmet baby food company in the country. Yuppies everywhere love her "Country Baby" products, and she's a big businesswoman again. But this time she doesn't go back to the rat race, partly because of the baby and partly because she's fallen in love with the local vet, Dr. Jeff Cooper, played by Sam Shepard.

There are certain parallels between J.C. Wiatt and Diane, as for some time Diane has been thinking about having children. The fact that six of her films in the eighties (not counting *Reds*, but including the 1988 *The Good Mother*) are concerned with some aspect of marriage, children, or not being able to have children, is an indication of how strong the maternal instinct is in her. But it was never as fully realized as it was in *Baby Boom*. For the first time in her life she was working closely with two very small children—the seventeen-month-old Kennedy twins who both played the thirteen-month-old Elizabeth because child labor laws allow a baby to be on the set for only two hours a day—and she found she took to it with a maternal ease. As someone who prepares exhaustively for any role, Diane went to see the babies every day, spending time alone with each of them for a couple of months before shooting started. It came to the point that when principal photography commenced she was their surrogate mother; during filming it was often Diane who could cajole the right reaction out of the babies by playing the clown with them or singing a lullaby to get them to sleep. Diane has said that it was "the most fun I've ever had" on a set and that she felt "completely relaxed with them," adding, "Because

I'm a big baby myself, I think we sort of understood each other."

Perhaps more enlightening is when Diane talks about how conducive they were to her performance. "It was great to be distracted by them because it forced me out of my own self-obsession and kept me spontaneous and alive." This sounds more like a woman describing her maternal instinct than an actress describing her craft. Diane's forty-first birthday occurred in the middle of shooting, and with this cathartic exposure to the babies she had to have wondered if it was getting too late for her to follow her maternal instinct. It's a big problem for women today; at some point the desire for independence and a career *has* to clash with an instinct so basically locked into womanhood. The final choice is, of course, something totally different and personal to each woman who has to face this question, but Diane must have had to face it head on in the role of J.C. Wiatt in *Baby Boom*.

Acting has been her life for the last twenty years, but judging from statements she has made during and after the filming of *Baby Boom* it seems quite manifest that the film gave her pause to question seriously whether she would like to have a child. Even before this, in an interview with Karen Heller in *USA Today* in late 1984, she had said, "I'd like to have a child. I think I can only have one child. Yeah, I think I'd like that very much." Two years later there was even more pressure on her, especially with the knowledge that many of her closest friends had families of one sort or another; the knowledge that Woody was starting a family with Mia could only have compounded the pressure. However, Diane is not a woman to have a baby just for the sake of it. She would only bear the child of someone she loved and was living with, although she hasn't ruled out the possibility of adopting a child. "I'm forty-one. I guess forty-five is kind of late. I'm all for marriage for the right reasons. I'm all for commitment, the good times shared, the helping each other through the tough times. I don't think, however, that you have to be married to have that kind of sustained relationship."

At this time Diane was in love with, and spending most of her time with, someone she loved, the actor Al Pacino. He was the third of her thespian loves. She is obviously, for the most part, attracted to actors, rather than people from other walks of life. "I couldn't imagine myself being involved with a doctor or a lawyer," she says. "They're too regimented. Also acting is a special life. You go here and you go there, and it's all so transitory. I think I'd always want to be with someone who understood that, someone who I could talk about work with. I think that's true for a lot of professions—you want to have something in common. I don't really think that opposites attract."

The transitory nature of acting that Diane talks about is obviously one of the reasons why she hasn't decided to have a child so far. It also brings out another identification between herself and the role of J.C.: that of dreaming for a home to escape to.

During the final filming of *Baby Boom* in the studio in Los Angeles, Diane, who has always dreamed of moving back to California, especially when vulnerable, alone, and insecure, nearly bought the old Ramon Novarro house in Los Feliz, an old part of Los Angeles, just below the Mount Wilson observatory. This time, it was less likely to be her search for security, given her then current love for Pacino, and more that she was having to spend a far greater part of the year in the movie capital with the various production projects she had going. And for someone who hates flying it seemed like a good idea to have a base on both coasts. For some reason—not because the house is said to be haunted by the ghost of the great silent star who was brutally murdered there twenty years ago— perhaps because she wanted to stay in New York near to Pacino and her friends in the city, she didn't buy the Egyptian *moderne* house. However, she is becoming more and more drawn to the Pacific Coast. During the winter of 1987, she spent a lot of time on a ranch outside Los Angeles that she rented when the Pacino affair started to go sour. And in the summer of 1988 she finally took the plunge and paid one point two million dollars for the Novarro house.

Yet New York and its hurly-burly pace is still the center of her life, with much to hold her here. She has her cats, her acting, dance, and gym classes, and it is the perfect place in the world for her to putter about the streets buying clothes, searching out memorabilia, visiting art galleries, going to the movies, and being able to walk on the streets virtually unrecognized. It would be detrimental to say that Diane's life is shopping, but it's undoubtedly one of her favorite pastimes. Joan Juliet Buck recalls that the day she interviewed Diane for *Vanity Fair* last year Diane couldn't resist picking up presents for three men: Mandy Patinkin, Kathryn Grody's husband; Marvin Heiferman, her collaborator on *Still Life*; and a fiftieth birthday present for Frederic Tuten, a professor of English who is also a friend. And this was all in the same West Side store!

Like J.C., Diane is in two minds about what she really wants—or, as Diane has seemed to be for much of her life, of two, three, or four minds, but that is the result of her inquisitive quest for ever-new avenues. She loves the bustle of New York just as much as she loves traveling the hinterland of the United States, the stark purity of the desert of Arizona and New Mexico, and the palm trees and blue waters of the Pacific Coast. Whether she would be entirely happy leaving New York is doubtful, and it is unlikely her new Los Feliz Oaks house will become her permanent home.

While people may consider her privileged lifestyle, which she has definitely earned, frivolous, there is another side to Diane that though less publicized is far more noble. It keeps her tied to New York on an altruistic level: her charity work with old people.

The death of Mary Alice Hall made a deep impression on her. She was as pivotal to Diane's life as her parents, Woody, and, perhaps, Warren. Right at the beginning of her career, while her parents may have supported her acting, it was her grandmother Mary Hall who got her back on her feet again when she went back to California defeated after her first set-backs. In an interview Diane did with *Interview* magazine in 1987 one senses the depth of Diane's love for her, and it's worth quoting her description in full, not just for her verbal portrait of Grammy Hall, but because it shows so much of Diane herself—how honest she is in her evaluations and how incisive she is in her observations:

> She was a brutally honest and extraordinarily beautiful woman. When I was a kid she was tough. I sort of grew into appreciating her. The spectacular thing about Mary was that she had this great sense of humor that was very Irish and sarcastic. You might think this crazy, but she reminded me of Jack Nicholson. She never trusted a soul in her life—not her son, not anyone. She raised my father alone. The story goes that her husband "died in a car accident." Then once I heard he "got sick." She lived all her life in a duplex in Highland Park. Grammy was very interested in money. It was her love in life. What is so bizarre about her is that she was a practicing Catholic all her life—yeah, she was a Catholic, yet she didn't "believe." She didn't believe there was a heaven. She was single minded in that respect; unlike other people, who convert toward the end of their lives, she didn't. She used to go to the grocery store with coupons, even though she had plenty of money. Sadie [Diane's great-aunt] died two years before Mary did. They were quite a team—living their lives together. They each had one son. Sadie didn't have her son, Charlie, until she was forty-three years old. So we're talking about quite an Irish pair. I mean, bingo every week, and going to Reno or Vegas every chance they could. She was a great character.

In certain respects Diane could be describing herself; certainly there are family resemblances, or at least things in Mary Hall's character that Diane admires.

It was shortly after Mary Hall's death that Diane took up volunteer work at the Jewish Home and Hospital for the Aged on 106th Street in Manhattan. Many of its residents have been involved in the entertainment business at one time or another, and Diane visits them every Tuesday evening she is in New York. Her descriptions of some of her regulars are filled with pathos and understanding. Some of them must be gone now, but to listen to Diane talk about such characters as Jack Shawn, an ex-art director at Columbia Pictures, who had problems during the McCarthy era for his socialist views, and Rose Cohen, who sees herself as a star and, incidentally, played the witch in the home's production of *The Wizard of Oz*, is extremely touching. On Thursday nights, the second evening of a seven-day week Diane gives up for the home, she helps with the weekly dance, and Diane lets the men lead her. Many of the people in the home don't even know who she is, which she finds refreshing. "It teaches you. It puts a lid on your grandiosity, and it makes you feel good about yourself."

This is a side of the reluctant star that hardly anyone sees, but it has great meaning to her life. Certainly it's a balance for the movie star who is aware of how pampered she could be if she were solely concerned with her public persona. "When you're acting in a movie, you're sort of like the prize pig. They cart you in to do the scenes. Then they throw you back in makeup and try to fix you up."

For the rest of 1987, after finishing *Baby Boom* in February, Diane didn't act like a "prize pig." She went back to being the anonymous person behind the camera. She had to finish supervising the post-production work on *Heaven* for its April release, and she was eager to get back to her on-going projects with Joe Kelly. It was announced that *The Lemon Sisters* was underway again, but that proved to be another false alarm, and their attention turned to *The Blue Angel*. Kelly and Keaton have obtained the rights to the 1930 Josef von Sternberg classic, which made Marlene Dietrich a star, as a vehicle for the singer Madonna, who Diane believes "contrary to popular belief, is a lot more like Dietrich than Marilyn Monroe." She hopes to get Alan Parker to direct the film from a new screenplay by Sarah Paley and Jarre Fees, although, as of this writing, nothing has been finalized yet. *The Blue Angel* is only one of several projects for which she and Kelly have a development deal with Twentieth Century Fox.

Much of the summer of 1987 was taken up with publicity for *Heaven* and *Baby Boom*. Usually reluctant to talk to the press, there was a spate of interviews and covers, including those for *Interview*, *Vanity Fair*, and Rupert Murdoch's new film magazine, *Premiere* (Murdoch also owns Twentieth Century Fox). She was more available to the press than at any time in her career, including 1977 with all the furor over *Annie Hall* and *Looking for Mr. Goodbar*. Diane even visited the Cannes Film Festival in May. However she was only concerned with the professional aspect of her life, promoting the two films, especially her own *Heaven*, and as usual, she was careful not to respond to questions about her private life, though inevitably they came up, especially about her relationship with Pacino.

This last relationship of hers was far more secret than her two more open relationships with Woody and Warren. Diane and Pacino were rarely seen in public together, even for important social functions such as the fiftieth anniversary of her alma mater, the Neighborhood Playhouse, which took place on December 3 at the Schubert Theater, when she returned to the boards again for the evening. Also performing with her in this gala evening of drama, dance, and music were other alumni, including Keir Dullea, Tammy Grimes, Anne Jackson, Louise Lasser, Tony Randall, Maureen Stapleton, Brenda Vaccaro, Gwen Verdon, Jon Voight, and Joanne Woodward. It was quite a cast for just one evening!

Meanwhile, *Baby Boom* had opened on October 7 to mostly wonderful reviews. Sometimes the plot was criticized for not being believable—but then how many comedy scenarios have ever been completely believable?—and writer Charles Shyer's second directorial effort wasn't as admired as his first

(Irreconcilable Differences). Diane's notices were almost unanimously good, with most critics saying that her performance
was the reason to see the film. As David Denby, not always
Diane's greatest advocate, put it in *New York*, "Yet the picture is
entertaining anyway—and at times entrancingly so—because
Diane Keaton is the lead. Returning to comedy after years of
dramatic roles, she has lost her dithering vagueness; she's brisk,
almost fierce, and she transforms the shopworn ideas into something ardent and fresh." Janet Maslin in *The New York Times* (for
once Canby didn't do the review) concurred, "Without Miss
Keaton—or even with Miss Keaton in one of her more fluttery
incarnations—none of this would be believable for a second.
Even so it isn't especially likely. But Miss Keaton's comically
exaggerated toughness and absurd self-confidence make the performance a delight. For an hour or so, at least, *Baby Boom* is
wicked enough to have real edge."

Her twentieth film was a personal triumph for Diane. Audiences flocked to see her, and by the very nature of the film it
was obvious that they were flocking to see *her*. The response to
Baby Boom confirmed that Diane is one of the most popular
actresses today. As *Film Comment* commented for its professional readership, "Delightful comedy about 'having it all' in the
eighties signals Diane Keaton's triumphant return to the ranks
of the screen's top comediennes."

If one could equate her talent and popularity to any other star
besides Carole Lombard it would have to be Katharine Hepburn, whose gifts and talent were preferred by the moviegoing
public in her comedy roles, especially with Spencer Tracy. Like
Hepburn, Diane is an intelligent and telling actress who prefers
to stretch herself however she can, evident in her choice of
roles. Sometimes these risks haven't succeeded, as Diane herself
says: "I think you ought to take a chance every single time you
go out and do something. If you continue to do things, I think
you're always amazed by what works and what doesn't. You
never know."

One thing we can be sure of is that Diane will keep extending

herself and experimenting, regardless of how the public per-
ceives her. She has too much courage to stick with the obvious.
Of all her many talents perhaps there is only one that she has
decided not to pursue in the future.

Audience reaction has put her off from singing in public. No
doubt this is because of the poor reception she received when
she tried her nightclub act for the first time in about eight years
at the Ice House in Pasadena and the American Place Theater in
Reno. She had delayed the Reno opening by one day (because
one of her dear friends had just been killed in an automobile
accident) which didn't please the audience. In both cities she
received dreadful reviews for her half-hour set which included
"You Made Me Love You," and it killed her first ambition for all
time. "In high school and college I had a fantasy that I'd have an
act and sing in a club. I tried, and boy, did I kill that dream. I
had the problem of being at the mercy of the audience. I was
thrown by everyone. Never again. Can you imagine me in
Vegas, kicking up my legs with a boy chorus in the background?" (Actually Miss Keaton, it sounds like it could be an
idea for a *very* funny film.)

Diane spent much of the winter of 1987–1988 out in Los Angeles working and seeing friends. Whether Pacino spent time
with her is difficult to determine, but their two-year affair was
already in trouble, and by the beginning of March 1988, it became known that they had split up. Apparently it was Diane's
decision, as she removed her things from Pacino's Hudson
County country house in upstate New York and, according to
friends, refused to take his calls. Pacino was acting at the Public
Theater in *Julius Caesar* when Diane made this final decision.
(Though it's not substantiated that she left him on the ides.)

So, at the beginning of her forty-second year, Diane was
alone again. What her problems were with Al Pacino is a more
closely guarded secret than those she had with Beatty. It is interesting to surmise that it might have had something to do with
wanting children, but that is only hearsay. In the aftermath,
Diane followed the unconscious pattern she established after the

breakups with Woody and Warren, and accepted a film role which would take her on location.

That she was hurt by the failure of this relationship can be seen in her remarks to Leslie Bennetts in an interview in the Sunday arts section of *The New York Times*, on June 26, 1988. "There's a good chance I won't ever marry. It looks like it. I believe it's a fine idea, but I don't know if it's going to happen to me, or if I'll participate enough in some situation that will make it happen." Yet Diane, ever the romantic, didn't rule out the question of falling in love with someone again: Obviously it's something she wishes for, but she's more realistic about it today. "Now I see it much more about accepting people for what they are and being less needy, and feeling less righteous about your neediness. I don't think it's easy, but that's what I think it is. I never really thought very sure about it in the past; it took me a long time to be able to think about me and my participation in it. I mean you think about what you want a lot, but not about what really is—and what you have to bring to it. Seeing things for what they are and yourself for what you are makes a big difference in what your expectations about what life is supposed to deliver you."

It is this vulnerable side of Diane, which she has never lost, that makes her so appealing to the public. Woody has said that she bares her soul in her acting, and it's absolutely true. Her openness and the truth in her acting allows everyone to identify and sympathize with her.

That she took on the role of Anna Dunlap in the film version of Sue Miller's controversial novel *The Good Mother* is yet another example of how willing she is to expose herself in her acting. Anna is a woman who falls obsessively in love with a younger man, who releases her sexuality for the first time in her life. Within the more open lifestyle she embraces, her daughter witnesses their making love, and the sculptor, Leo, allows the four-year-old girl to touch his genitals once when he comes out of the shower. In the resulting custody battle with her ex-husband Anna loses her daughter and her life is destroyed. It's a harrowing role, and while she may have found working on location in Toronto easier than staying in New York, where she would be physically closer to Pacino and therefore more vulnerable to the effects of leaving him, to play this role was not running away.

Diane's reaction on first hearing about *The Good Mother* was to say to director Leonard Nimoy, especially when she read the script and found that she was required to do explicit love scenes, which have always given her trouble, "Just *forget* it!—I mean people are just going to go, 'Take her off the *screen!* We don't want to *see* her!'" But, eventually, she agreed to do it, and in the role she has had to express a woman coming to terms with her sexuality, falling in love, and losing her child.

Advance word on *The Good Mother* was good indeed. The film was eagerly awaited due to a flood of pre-publicity throughout the late summer and early fall of 1988 prior to its release date on November 4. The word was out that Diane's performance would get her a third Oscar nomination, and this in a year of very strong leading female performances.

Unfortunately *The Good Mother* proved not to be up to expectations. The power of Sue Miller's book just simply didn't come across in the screen adaptation, mainly because the story had been sanitized for mass consumption, and most of the reviews were lukewarm at best. Diane's performance was praised by some; *Sneak Previews* was quoted "The finest performance by any actress so far this year"; WABC-TV's Joel Siegal called it "Diane Keaton's finest performance since *Annie Hall*," and David Denby, even though he didn't like the film, wrote in *New York* magazine, "*The Good Mother* would be unimaginable without Diane Keaton, who once again brings a clarifying anger and a stumbling but powerful sense of discovery to the struggles of a woman beginning to enjoy herself sexually." But such influential publications as *The Hollywood Reporter* called Diane's acting "erratic" and Janet Maslin in *The New York Times* was even less enthusiastic about Diane's portrayal of Anna, suggesting she never made the role believable.

Perhaps the most favorable review of all came from *Daily Variety*, but as a trade paper this wasn't seen by the public, and the damage was done. After four weeks on 104 screens across the country, the film had only grossed $4½ million.

Much of the problem lay in the script, which was too tame and did little to accentuate the drama of the relationships and situation. It is only at the end, when Anna's world has fallen apart that Diane really gets a chance to show what she is capable of, and the two last scenes are very powerful indeed.

In the meantime, Diane had gone on to another project, and this one is very dear to her heart. Finally, she and Joe Kelly had found the backing for their long-delayed project, *The Lemon Sisters*. Shooting started in Atlantic City on September 27, 1988, with Joyce Chopra directing Diane, Carol Kane, Kathryn Grody, Ruben Blades, Aidan Quinn, and Elliott Gould.

The Lemon Sisters not only marks Diane's debut as a producer of a feature film, but also her return to singing, dancing, and acting, just as she started her career twenty years before. When the film comes out in 1989 it will be interesting to see just how far she has progressed since *Hair*.

This is what makes Diane so exceptional as an actress. She continually stretches herself in the roles she chooses, and gives all of herself to the audiences in her acting. Which makes it all the more surprising that she is genuinely unaware of the impact she has made through her films. Perhaps this is best illustrated in a closing remark she made to Joan Juliet Buck in *Vanity Fair*, "I do agree with Borges that we may all be in a dog's dream." In this case she was referring to heaven, but it sounds more like a philosophy of life . . . and very Allenesque.

In the last nineteen years Diane has made twenty-two films. In at least seven, her performances were regarded as some of the finest screen acting ever seen. Regardless of what she will go on to do next—whether it be a film project with Joe Kelly, or another astounding portrayal of a difficult role—she has left her mark. Diane was recently quoted, in one of the few instances she has let down the guard on her personal feelings, that she was enormously comforted by Mary Hall's grave, which she has visited many times. This earthly proof of Mary's existence means something to her, because it's an outward sign that Mary will be remembered.

Yet Mary has already been immortalized in Woody's cinematic love poem to Diane, *Annie Hall*. Likewise, whatever artistic or personal mountains Diane goes on to conquer, she is already immortalized in the minds of many people as one of the finest comediennes in the history of film who, sometimes even wearing the same hat, can give depth, subtlety, and total reality to the most heart-rending dramatic roles.

Perhaps Woody sums up her talents best, when he insists, without, he says, any prejudice, that she is one of the great film actresses of all time, far better than any of the stars of the golden age of Hollywood or the present:

Nobody has her varied range. Nobody can play comedy like she can, broad comedy where you hit her on the head and sophisticated light comedy. But she can also play intense drama like O'Neill or Strindberg and go onstage and sing beautifully and dance if she has to.

Filmography

Lovers and Other Strangers

Directed by Cy Howard; screenplay by Renee Taylor, Joseph Bologna, and David Z. Goodman; director of photography, Andy Laszio; music by Fred Karlin; produced by David Suskind. With Bea Arthur, Bonnie Bedella, Michael Brandon, Richard Castellano, Bob Dishy, Harry Guardino, Marian Hailey, Joseph Hindy, Anthony Holland, Anne Jackson, *Diane Keaton*, Cloris Leachman, Mort Marshall, Anne Meara, Gig Young (Cinerama Releasing Corporation, 106 mins., opened August 13, 1970).

The Godfather

Directed by Francis Ford Coppola; screenplay by Mario Puzo and Mr. Coppola, based on the novel by Mr. Puzo; director of photography, Gordon Willis; editors, William Reynolds and Peter Zinner; music composed by Nino Rota; produced by Albert S. Ruddy. With Marlon Brando, Al Pacino, James Caan, Richard Castellano, Robert Duvall, Sterling Hayden, John Conte, *Diane Keaton*, Al Lettieri, Abe Vigoda, Talia Shire, Gianni Russo, John Cazale, Rudy Bond, Al Martino, Morgana King (Paramount Pictures, 175 mins., opened March 15, 1972).

Play It Again, Sam

Directed by Herbert Ross; screenplay by Woody Allen, based on his Broadway play; photography by Owen Roizman; edited by Marion Rothman; produced by Arthur P. Jacobs. With Woody Allen, *Diane Keaton*, Jerry Lacy, Susan Anspach,

Jennifer Salt, Joy Bang, Viva (Paramount Pictures, 78 mins., opened May 5, 1972).

S l e e p e r

Directed by Woody Allen; screenplay by Mr. Allen and Marshall Brickman; director of photography, David Walsh; editor, Ralph Rosenblum; produced by Jack Grossberg; executive producer, Charles H. Joffe. With Woody Allen, *Diane Keaton*, John Beck, Marya Small, Bartiett Robinson, Mary Gregory (United Artists, 88 mins., opened December 18, 1973).

The Godfather, Part II

Produced and directed by Francis Ford Coppola; screenplay by Mr. Coppola and Mario Puzo, based on Mr. Puzo's novel, *The Godfather*; co-produced by Gary Frederickson and Fred Roos; director of photography, Gordon Willis; music by Nino Rota; editors, Peter Zinner, Barry Malkin, Richard Marks. With Al Pacino, Robert Duvall, *Diane Keaton*, Robert De Niro, John Cazale, Talia Shire, Lee Strasberg, Michael V. Gazzo, G.D. Spradlin, Richard Bright, Gaston Moschin, B. Kirby Jr., Morgana King, James Caan (Paramount Pictures, 200 mins., opened December 13, 1974).

Love and Death

Written and directed by Woody Allen; produced by Charles H. Joffe; executive producer, Martin Poll; music by Sergei A. Prokofiev; edited by Ralph Rosenblum; director of photography, Ghislain Cloquet; a Jack Rollins and Charles H. Joffe production. With Woody Allen, *Diane Keaton*, Feodor Atkine, Yves Barsaacq, Lloyd Battista, Brian Coburn, Herny Czarniak, Despo Diamantidou, Olga Georges-Picot, Jessica Harper, Leib Lensky, Alfred Lutter 3d, Zvee Scooler, James Tolkan, Harold Gould (United Artists, 89 mins., opened June 11, 1975).

I Will, I Will ... For Now

Directed by Norman Panama; written by Mr. Panama and Albert E. Lewin; director of photography, John A. Alonzo; music by John Cameron; produced by George Barrie. With Elliott Gould, *Diane Keaton*, Paul Sorvino, Victoria Principal, Robert Alda, Warren Berlinger, Candy Clark, Madge Sinclair, Carmen Zapata, George Tyne, Koko Tani, Sheila Rogers, Michele Clinton, Lou Tiano (20th Century-Fox, 107 mins., opened February 19, 1976).

Harry and Walter Go to New York

Directed by Mark Rydell; screenplay by John Byrum and Robert Kaufman, based on a story by Don Devlin and Mr. Byrum; executive producer, Tony Bill; produced by Mr. Devlin and Harry Gittes; director of photography, Laszlo Kovacs; music by David Shire; supervising film editor, Fredric Steinkamp; editors, David Bretherton and Don Guldice. With James Caan, Elliott Gould, Michael Caine, *Diane Keaton*, Charles Durning, Leslie Ann Warren, Val Avery, Jack Gilford, Dennis Dugan, Carol Kane, Kathryn Grody, David Proval, Michael Conrad, Burt Young, Bert Ramsen (Columbia Pictures, 123 mins., opened June 18, 1976).

Annie Hall

(Academy Award for Best Actress, Golden Globe, New York Film Critics, and National Film Critics Awards for Best Actress)

Directed by Woody Allen; screenplay by Woody Allen and Marshall Brickman; director of photography, Gordon Willis; editor, Ralph Rosenblum; produced by Charles H. Joffe, executive producer, Robert Greenhut. With Woody Allen, *Diane Keaton*, Tony Roberts, Carol Kane, Paul Simon, Colleen Dewhurst, Shelley Duvall, Janet Margolin, Christopher Walken, Donald Symington, Helen Ludlam, Mordecai Lawner, Joan

Newman, Jonathan Munk, Ruth Volner, Martin Rosenblatt, Hy Ansel, Rashel Novikoff, Russell Horton, Marshall McLuhan, Dick Cavett, Christine Jones, Mary Boylan, Wendy Gerard, John Doumanian (United Artists, 94 mins., opened April 21, 1977).

Looking for Mr. Goodbar

Directed by Richard Brooks; screenplay by Mr. Brooks, based on the novel by Judith Rossner; director of photography, William A. Fraker; editor, George Grenville; music by Artie Kane; produced by Freddie Fields. With *Diane Keaton*, Tuesday Weld, William Atherton, Richard Kiley, Richard Gere, Alan Feinstein, Tom Berenger, Priscilla Pointer, Laurie Prange, Joel Fabiani, Julius Harris, Richard Bright (Paramount Pictures, 136 mins., opened October 20, 1977).

Interiors

Written and directed by Woody Allen; director of photography, Gordon Willis; edited by Ralph Rosenblum; produced by Charles H. Joffe. With Kristin Griffith, Marybeth Hurt, Richard Jordan, *Diane Keaton*, E.G. Marshall, Geraldine Page, Maureen Stapleton, Sam Waterston (United Artists, 99 mins., opened August 2, 1978).

Manhattan

Directed by Woody Allen; Written by Mr. Allen and Marshall Brickman; director of photography, Gordon Willis; production designer, Mel Bourne; costumes, Albert Wolsky; edited by Susan E. Morse; music by George Gershwin, performed by the New York Philharmonic, conducted by Zubin Mehta, and the Buffalo Philharmonic, conducted by Michael Tilson Thomas; executive producer, Robert Greenhut; produced by Charles H. Joffe. A Jack Rollins-Charles H. Joffe production. With Woody Allen, *Diane Keaton*, Michael Murphy, Mariel

Hemingway, Meryl Streep, Anne Byrne, Karen Ludwug, Michael O'Donahue, Victor Truro, Tisa Farrow, Helen Hanft, Bella Abzug, Gary Weiss, Kenny Vance, Charles Levin, Karen Allen, David Rasche, Damion Sheller, Wallace Shawn, Mark Lynn Baker, Frances Conroy, Bill Anthony, John Doumanian, Ray Serra (United Artists, 96 mins., opened April 25, 1979).

Reds

(Academy Award Nomination for Best Actress)

Produced and Directed by Warren Beatty; executive producers, Simon Relph and Dede Allen; associate producer, David MacLeod; screenplay by Warren Beatty and Trevor Griffiths; director of photography, Vittorio Storaro; edited by Dede Allen and Craig McKay; production design by Richard Sylbert; costume design by Shirley Russell; music by Steven Sondheim and Dave Grusin. With Warren Beatty, *Diane Keaton*, Jack Nicholson, Edward Herrmann, Jerzy Kosinski, Paul Sorvino, Maureen Stapleton, Nicholas Coster, M. Emmet Walsh, Ian Wolfe, Bessie Love, MacIntyre Dixon, Pat Starr, Eleanor D. Wilson, Max Wright, George Plimpton, Harry Ditson, Leigh Curran, Kathryn Grody, Belinda Currin, Nancy Duiguid, Norman Chancer, Dolf Sweet, Ramon Bieri, Jack O'Leary, Gene Hackman, William Daniels, Dave King, Joseph Buloff, Josef Sommer, R.G. Armstrong (Paramount Pictures, 199 mins., opened December 3, 1981).

Shoot the Moon

Directed by Alan Parker; written by Bo Goldman; director of photography, Michael Seresin; edited by Gerry Hambling; produced by Alan Marshall. With Albert Finney, *Diane Keaton*, Karen Allen, Peter Weller, Dana Hill, Viveka Davis, Tracey Gold, Tina Yothers, George Murdock, Leora Dana, Irving Metzman, Kenneth Kimmins, Michael Aldredge, Robert Costanzo (Metro-Goldwin-Mayer, 123 mins., opened January 22, 1982).

The Little Drummer Girl

Directed by George Roy Hill; screenplay by Loring Mandel, based on the novel by John le Carré; director of photography, Wolfgang Treu; edited by William Reynolds; music by David Grusin; produced by Robert L. Crawford. With *Diane Keaton*, Yorgo Voyagis, Klaus Kinski, Sami Frey, Michael Cristofer, David Suchet, Eli Danker (Warner Bros., 131 mins., opened October 19, 1984).

Mrs. Soffel

Directed by Gillian Armstrong; written by Ron Nyswaner; production design by Luciana Arrighi; director of photography, Russell Boyd; music by Mark Isham; edited by Nicholas Beauman; produced by Edgar J. Scherick, Scott Rudin and David A. Nicksay. With *Diane Keaton*, Mel Gibson, Matthew Modine, Edward Herrmann, Trini Alvarado, Jenni Dundass, Danny Corkill, Harley Cross, Terry O'Quinn, Pippa Pearthree, William Youmans, Maury Chaykin, Joyce Ebert, John W. Carroll, Dana Wheeler-Nicholson, Wayne Robson, Les Rubie, Paula Trueman (MGM/UA, 110 mins., opened December 23, 1984).

Crimes of the Heart

Directed by Bruce Beresford; screenplay by Beth Henley, based on her play; director of photography, Dante Spinotti; edited by Anne Goursaud; music by Georges Delerue; produced by Freddie Fields. With *Diane Keaton*, Jessica Lange, Sissy Spacek, Sam Shepard, Tess Harper, David Carpenter, Hurd Hatfield, Beeson Carroll, Jean Willard, Tom Mason, Gregory Travis, Annie McKnight (De Laurentiis Entertainment Group, 105 mins., opened December 12, 1986).

Radio Days

Written and directed by Woody Allen; director of photography, Carlo Di Palma; edited by Susan E. Morse, produced by

Robert Greenhut. With Danny Aiello, Jeff Daniels, Mia Farrow, Seth Green, Robert Joy, Julie Kavner, *Diane Keaton*, Julie Kurnitz, Renee Lippin, Kenneth Mars, Josh Mostel, Tony Roberts, Wallace Shawn, Michael Tucker, David Warrilow, Dianne Wiest, Woody Allen, Belle Berger, Joel Eidelsberg, Tito Puente (Orion Pictures, 90 mins., opened January 30, 1987).

Heaven

Directed by *Diane Keaton*; cinematography by Frederick Elmes and Joe Kelly; edited by Paul Barnes; art direction, Barbara Ling; music by Howard Shore; produced by Joe Kelly; executive producers, Tom Kuhn, Charles Mitchell, and Arlyne Rothberg (Island Pictures, 80 mins., opened March 25, 1987).

Baby Boom

Directed by Charles Shyer; written by Nancy Meyers and Mr. Shyer; director of photography, William A. Faker; editor, Lynzee Klingman; music by Bill Conte; production designer, Jeffrey Howard; costume designer, Susan Becker; produced by Miss Meyers. With *Diane Keaton*, Sam Shepard, Harold Ramis, Sam Wanamaker, James Spader, Pat Hingle, Kristina and Michelle Kennedy (United Artists Pictures, 103 mins., opened October 7, 1987).

The Good Mother

Directed by Leonard Nimoy; screenplay by Martin Bortman, based on the novel by Sue Miller; director of photography, David Watkin; film editor, Peter Berger; music by Elmer Bernstein; production designer, Stan Jolley; produced by Arnold Glimcher. With *Diane Keaton*, Liam Neeson, Jason Robards, Ralph Belamy, Teresa Wright, James Naughton, Asia Vieira, Joe Morton, Katey Sagal (Touchstone, 104 mins., opened November 4, 1988).

The Lemon Sisters

Directed by Joyce Chopra; music, Paul Schaffer; cinematography, Bobby Byrne; costumes, Susan Becker; production design, Patrizia Von Brandenstein; executive producers, Tom Kuhn and Charles Mitchell; produced by *Diane Keaton* and Joe Kelly. With *Diane Keaton*, Carol Kane, Kathryn Grody, Ruben Blades, Aidan Quinn, Elliott Gould (Miramax Films, due 1989).

THEATRICAL PERFORMANCES
New York

Hair

Biltmore Theater, opened April 29, 1968. Diane in the role of Parent. Took over the lead of Sheila in October 1968.

Play It Again, Sam

Broadhurst Theater, opened February 12, 1969. Closed March 14, 1970.

Primary English Class

Downtown Circle in the Square, opened February 7, 1976. Closed May 16, 1976.

Bibliography

BOOKS

Allen, Woody.   *Play It Again, Sam*, Random House 1969.
Getting Even, Random House 1971.
Without Feathers, Random House 1975.
Side Effects, Random House, 1980.

Bach, Steven.   *Final Cut*, William Morrow & Co., 1985.

Brode, Douglas.   *Woody Allen, His Films and Career*, Lyle Stuart, 1985.

Collins, Joan.   *Past Imperfect, An Autobiography*, Simon & Schuster, 1978, 1984.

Cronin, Vincent.   *Catherine, Empress of All the Russias*, William Morrow & Co., 1978.

De Navacelle, T.   *Woody Allen on Location*, William Morrow & Co., 1979.

Keaton, Diane (with Marvin Heiferman).   *Reservations*, Alfred, A. Knopf, Inc., 1980.
Still Life, Simon & Schuster, 1983.

Knight, Vivianne.   *Trevor Howard, A Gentleman and a Player*, Beaufort Books, 1986.

Munshower, Suzanne.   *The Diane Keaton Scrapbook*, Grosset & Dunlap, 1979.
Warren Beatty, His Life, His Loves, His Work, St. Martin's Press, 1983.

Reed, John.   *The Ten Days That Shook the World*, Boni & Liveright, 1919.

Thomson, David.   *Warren Beatty and Desert Eyes*, Double-day & Co., Inc., 1987.

Wiley, Mason and
Bona, Damien.   *Inside Oscar, The Unofficial History of the Academy Awards*, Ballantine, 1988.

ARTICLES

Bennetts, Leslie, "Diane Keaton Grapples With Maternity," *The New York Times*, June 26, 1988.

Brown, Gloria, "Mother Load," *Seven Days*, November 9, 1988.

Buck, Joan Juliet, "Inside Diane Keaton," *Vanity Fair*, March 1987.

Canby, Vincent, "When Coyness Becomes a Cop-Out: Risking It Without Laughs," August, 1978.

Canby reviews, *Play It Again, Sam, The New York Times*, May 5, 1972; *Shoot the Moon*, January 22, 1982; *Interiors*, August 2, 1978; *Manhattan*, April 25, 1979.

Counts, Kyle, *The Good Mother, Hollywood Reporter*, November 3, 1988.

Daily Variety, The Good Mother, November 1, 1988.

Davis, Daphne, "Warren Beatty: Self-Love Conquers All," *Cue*, August 18, 1978.

Dunne, Dominick, "Diane Keaton" *Vanity Fair*, 1985.

Edelstein, David, "Love and Loss," *New York Post*, November 4, 1988.

Flatley, Guy, "Interiors," *The New York Times*, October 21, 1977.

Herschberg, Lynn, "Keaton Talks Funny" *Premiere*, October 1987.

The Hollywood Reporter, "The Week at the Boxoffice," December 6, 1988.

L'Ecuyer, Gerald, "Diane Keaton," *Interview*, January 1987.

Maslin, Janet, "Interiors—The Dark Side of Annie Hall," *The New York Times*, August, 1978.

Maslin reviews *The Good Mother*, *The New York Times*, November 4, 1988.

Rochlin, Margy, "All In The Family," *Premiere*, October 1987.

Schaeffer, Steven, "Keaton's a Mom Again," *Boston Herald*, November 1, 1988.

Stephan Schiff, "Woody's Comic Wail," *Boston Phoenix*, May 8, 1979.

Wong, Wayman, "Good Mother, Bad Movie," *New York Daily News*, November 13, 1988.

INDEX